THE UNIVERSAL BACH

Lectures Celebrating the Tercentenary of
Bach's Birthday

Fall 1985

American Philosophical Society
Independence Square • Philadelphia

Library of Congress Catalog Card No. 86-071071
International Standard Book No. 0-87169-436-0

Contents

Foreword
   Martin A. Heckscher vii

Musical and Numerical Symbolism
   in the Large Choral Works:
   Bach's Secret Code
   Michael Korn 1

The Articulation of Genre in
   Bach's Instrumental Music
   Laurence Dreyfus 10

Bach the Cantor, the Capellmeister,
   and the Musical Scholar:
   Aspects of the *B-Minor Mass*
   Christoph Wolff 39

On Bach's Universality
   Robert L. Marshall 50

Bach as Biblical Interpreter
   Richard L. Jeske 82

Contributors

Michael Korn
Artistic Director
Basically Bach Festival

Laurence Dreyfus
Assistant Professor of the History of Music
Yale University

Christoph Wolff
Professor of Music
Harvard University

Robert L. Marshall
Professor of Music
Brandeis University

Richard L. Jeske
Professor of New Testament
Lutheran Theological Seminary

Foreword

This volume published with the cooperation and generosity of the American Philosophical Society is a fitting commemorative of the Basically Bach Festival's celebration of the 300th anniversary of the birth of Johann Sebastian Bach.

The Festival was organized by a small committee in the Chestnut Hill section of Philadelphia in 1976. Since the Festival's first concert at St. Paul's Church on October 15, 1976, the intention of its organizers and Artistic Director, Michael Korn, has been to present primarily the works of Bach, but also of other composers from the Baroque era, in performances of the highest quality in settings appropriate to the music, such as churches and museums. As early as 1978 the *Philadelphia Inquirer* observed that the Festival "... has already achieved the status of a major music festival."

During its ten seasons the Festival has enjoyed a close relationship with the community of Chestnut Hill. Many of the Festival's events have been held in Chestnut Hill with St. Paul's Church, the Church of St. Martin-in-the-Fields and the Woodmere Art Gallery as the principal locations. During the first five years the Chestnut Hill Community Fund was used as a conduit for funding; in addition, Chestnut Hill businesses have supported the Festival in a variety of ways.

In recent years events have been held in other locations, such as Center City and the Main Line. The lecture series published in this volume was presented in the Library of the American Philosophical Society, an appropriate location for these scholarly offerings. While the concerts in the early years were attended by audiences principally from Chestnut Hill, the Festival now attracts music lovers from the entire Delaware Valley and well beyond. Nevertheless, the Festival has recently renewed its commitment to Chestnut Hill as its focus in order to maintain the atmosphere of a European music festival.

In 1981 the Festival underwent several major changes. It incorporated and qualified as a publicly supported organization under section 501(c)(3) of the Internal Revenue Code. Also, the Festival hired its first staff member, Mary Sue Welsh, who has ably filled the position of Executive Director for five years.

In each of its ten years the Festival has included one of Bach's major choral works as its centerpiece: The *Mass in B Minor* occupied this position for six seasons and each of the *Passions* for two. In 1981 the Festival, which is held in mid-autumn, expanded to six programs extending over several weeks. In 1983 the *Christmas Oratorio* was offered in December, and by now a concert during the Christmas season appears to have become a firmly established tradition.

Since the outset The Concerto Soloists of Philadelphia and The Philadelphia Singers have provided the instrumental and choral forces for the larger works. As part of its commitment to musical performances of the highest quality, the Festival has also presented instrumental and vocal soloists of national and international standing. In 1984 Marie Claire Alain played Bach's 18 "Great" Chorale Preludes (Leipzig) on the organ of the Bryn Mawr Presbyterian Church in a unique program in which The Philadelphia Singers sang the same chorales. Other guest artists have included Ralph Kirkpatrick, Sergiu Luca, Anner Bylsma, Charles Bressler, Jon Humphrey, Gary Kendall and Lionel Rogg. The Festival has declined to take sides in the musicological debate over "original" versus "modern" instruments. While most works have been performed on the latter, the two types of instruments have been used together on occasion, and in recent years the Festival program has included at least one concert by an original instruments ensemble such as Aston Magna or The Bach Ensemble.

Several years ago the Festival began preparing for Bach's Tercentenary. The outcome was a year-long presentation of Bach's genius in keeping with the Festival's highest expectations. Included among the musical offerings were a gala benefit and national telecast on 19 June of "A Celebration for Handel and Bach" in cooperation with WHYY, the Pennsylvania Academy of the Fine Arts, The Philadelphia Singers and The Concerto Soloists and funded by the Mabel Pew Myrin Trust, IU International and the William Penn Foundation. During the spring Mr. Korn expanded the educational element of the Festival by giving demonstration lectures at four inner city Philadelphia high schools. On 24 November a free concert was held at The Philadelphia Museum of Art in conjunction with the opening of a special exhibition which included the Scheide portrait of Bach and other memorabilia. The Festival itself expanded to seven concerts in a series covering the scope of Bach's work which was entitled "The Universal Bach." The major works, with which the lectures in the present volume were interspersed, included the *St. Matthew Passion* and the complete *Motets, Brandenburg Concertos* and *Christmas Oratorio.*

In closing, we are deeply grateful to the American Philosophical Society for publishing this volume. The 1985 Festival was truly a milestone in the fulfillment of its organizers' dreams—to present Bach's achievements to the village of Chestnut Hill, to the entire Delaware Valley and ultimately to the nation and the world as part of an annual event that bears the unmistakable stamp of artistic authenticity and validity.

Martin A. Heckscher, President
The Basically Bach Festival
of Philadelphia

Musical and Numerical Symbolism in the Large Choral Works: Bach's Secret Code

Michael Korn

or those of you who have heard me lecture in the past, you will perhaps recall that my topic has usually been related in some manner to the concurrent festival. This year, first because of the distinguished array of scholars who will follow after me here at the Philosophical Society, and, secondly, with an awareness that these words are slated for publication—a prospect a bit horrifying for me in that I'm accustomed to performing and not to having my words frozen in print—I'm walking with trepidation on my subject, one that looked a lot simpler this summer before I really took it all down and began to organize my thoughts.

My topic then, and one that has become something of an obsession, I call "Bach's secret code": the numbers, the numerological significance behind the large choral works and the musical symbolism that played a part in them as well. But first, perhaps it would be wise to state why I believe this to be special to Bach, and why it seems to happen above all in the works dating from the last 25 years of his life.

To begin with, from the purely practical standpoint Bach's final quarter century found him in Leipzig, in the position of Kantor of the Thomaskirche. And as "Cantor zu St. Thomae et Director Musices Lipsiensis" Bach was the single most important musician of the town, in charge of music for the four major churches in Leipzig (the Thomaskirche, the Nicolaikirche, the Matthaeikirche, and the Petrikirche) for which he was empowered to call on pupils of the choir school attached to the Thomaskirche. Above all, his duties called for the composition of choral music, and lots of it, a feat Bach accomplished at oftentime amazing speed. And the words, the texts set in these pieces, particularly Biblical texts, seemed to have inspired Bach to look for something profound, an other-worldly quality that he invested in his music.

For me, this other-worldly dimension relates sizably to Bach's interest in numerology, not especially surprising if one bears in mind his view of music and its links to the world at large. It is a belief that has been around for a rather long time. For the ancient Greeks it was thought of as something common to the activities concerned with the pursuit of truth and beauty. Indeed, in the teaching of Pythagoras, music and arithmetic were not at all separate; just as the understanding of numbers was thought to be the key to comprehending the dual realms of the spiritual and the physical, so too the system of music could be ordered by numbers. Or, on a vastly different plane, consider that Richard Wagner was born in the year 1813, died on February 13, and wrote 13 operas (his name likewise contains 13 letters). In the case of Bach, based on the old Thamudenic Greek alphabet, with $A = 1$, $B = 2$, and so on, Bach equals the number 14; J.S. Bach $= 41$. These things, one might say, are part of the universe, part of God's grand plan, and Bach, I think, believed himself part of this—a reality reflected again and again in his vocal music composed in Leipzig.

I have attempted to categorize the different types of numerological symbolism employed by Bach as witnessed in the large choral works along with two cantatas to demonstrate my points, although what I will talk about crops up in many other compositions, noticeably the later cantatas. Inextricably bound with this is the fact that the name Bach—"B" "A" "C" "H"—spells out a melody that has worked its way into a wide variety of pieces (in the works of Bach as well as of other composers): "B" being *B* flat, in German; "A", *A* natural; "C", *C* natural; and "H", again in German, *B* natural. So we find this theme occurring also as a musical motive in addition to its numerological significance throughout Bach's *oeuvre*. Furthermore, we can say that of the individual parts comprising the whole, four minus one is three—in turn the Trinity; four plus one equals five—the books of Moses; four signifies the Four Gospels; one, the indivisible divine creator, God. And so, even within the number 14, standing for "B" "A" "C" "H," there are cross relations, by no means exhausted by the examples cited here.

In the final organ chorale, *Vor deinen Thron' tret ich hiermit* (BWV 668), the first part of the chorale tune is fashioned in 14 notes, the entire tune in 41 notes. Thus even at the end of his life, Bach was depicting himself standing before his creator. In this way he con-sciously interjects his own personality, as if to say "I believe in this also," almost in the same spirit as a renaissance painter who, rather than signing his name on a work, includes somewhere within the canvas his own likeness.

The motet *Fürchte dich nicht, ich bin bei dir* (BWV 228, "Be not afraid, I am with thee") reveals a division according to a symmetrical design where 77 measures are allotted to the first half and another 77 to the second. Now, not only do we have an architectual struc-ture, but Bach employs the number 77 to express seven plus seven equaling 14 on the first side and seven plus seven equaling 14 on the other. To add to the symbolism, when we reach the midpoint at the moment where the text turns to baptism and reads "Fear not, for I have redeemed thee, I have called thee by name," Bach uses as the basis of the fugato the notes spelling out his own name, implying that he, Bach, has been called by name. Not only does Bach layer this in numbers, but he puts in his name musically as well. A similar thing takes place at the end of the *St. Matthew Passion,* when just after the crucifixion, the stunned believers standing around the cross utter "Wahrlich, dieser ist Gottes sohn, gewesen" ("Truly this was the Son of God"). Of course, we hear this as one of the emotional highpoints of the Passion. What we don't usually notice is that under this, the basses of the chorus are singing 14 notes, yet another affirmation by Bach that he too believes.

As it relates to the symbolism of the Trinity we encounter many times the number 27: the Trinity times the Trinity—3 times 3 times 3. It is this number that appears to have obsessed Bach in the justly famous cantata BWV 4, *Christ lag in Todes Banden* ("Christ lay in the Chains of Death"). In beginning with a sinfonia comprising 14 measures Alfred Dürr, the eminent Bach scholar, saw the possibility that the work could have been the composer's first cantata. The first movement, a fugato Alleluja, is 27 measures in length and the interval of the third plays a prominent part as well. The second movement is divided into two parts, the first lasting 26 bars, the second 27, and thus it is the 27th bar that marks the division of the two halves. In the third movement, at bar 27, in the middle of an allegro, the music breaks into an adagio at the moment the text turns to the imagery of death. And in the fifth movement, again at bar 27, Bach adds two bars to the bass line when the text refers to the sacrifice of Christ's death changing the course of the world.

Interest in the Trinity in my estimation reaches its culmination in the *"Sanctus"* of the *B Minor Mass*, the earliest compositional layer of the Mass, dating from 1724, within a year of Bach's taking up his position in Leipzig. Not only does the *"Sanctus"* appear with all its rhythmic activity restricted to triplets (signifying the Trinity), but the orchestra is grouped into three sets of three, denoting therefore the Trinity squared (three times three times three)—three trumpets, three oboes, and first and second violins plus viola. From the same work it obviously did not escape Bach that the word "Credo" has added interest when equated with its numerical equivalency of 43. And related as well to the Credo, it may be noted here that there are 43 days between Maundy Thursday and Ascension. And so when Christ prophesied at the Last Supper that he would return to his disciples, the lapse in time was 43 days. As the individual letters of "Credo" yield 43 Bach responds by having the word appear 43 times during the length of the movement. But not quite. Actually it is heard only 39 times during the "Credo." If we turn to the "Patrem omnipotentem" it may be observed that the word "Credo" appears four more times, dissolving little by little into the new text of the new movement. In the *St. Matthew Passion's* depiction of the Last Supper, when Jesus sings of the Resurrection, we find 43 notes in the continuo leading up to the revelation of the union Jesus will have with his disciples in heaven.

Of the cantatas it may be said that the majority are laid out according to a triangular configuration related again to the Trinity. More often than not the cantatas are arranged in seven movements, all of which usually relate in a cross-wise arrangement working toward this pyramid wherein the turning point, or climax, is the fourth movement. The first movement and seventh are related in that the former is generally a chorus and the latter a chorale; the second relates to the sixth movement as both are for vocal solo; the third to the fifth movement, again both solo movements; and the fourth, at the apex of the triangle, most often a chorus that reveals the moral of the work. And its story is predominantly the trials and tribulations of the Christian's life progressing on the opening side of the triangle with the resolution of all this by heavenly redemption on the other side. Bach extends this in the "Credo" of the *B-Minor Mass* by adding even more movements so that now we have nine forming a vastly enlarged inverted triangle with the "Crucifixus" standing at the bottom, the first and ninth movement at the top both set as choruses, the second and eighth again choruses, the third and seventh movements arias, the fourth and sixth choruses, and finally, at the bottom of the inverted triangle, the "Crucifixus," the scene of the crucifixion. On either side of this is the "Et incarnatus est" wherein it is revealed Christ descended from heaven, and on the other side the "Et resurrexit" with Christ ascending to heaven. In this way the music forms an architectural structure of symbolic import. Bach takes this even further in the motet *Jesu, meine Freude* (BWV 227, "Jesus, my joy") where there are now eleven movements with the five-part fugal sixth movement as the center-piece. Another layer of symbolism employed here concerning num-bers is that all the even-numbered movements are taken from the scripture of St. Paul, chapter 8, and all of the odd numbers from the text of the chorale.

I now turn to a form of symbolism known at least from the Renaissance termed *Augenmusik*, "eye music." It is a kind of sym-bolism that is only seen by looking at the notes on the page. With Bach this might cleverly coincide, if it is vocal music, with the word *Kreuz* (cross) and another kind of *Kreuz*, a sharp sign before a note, indicating that it be chromatically raised. (During Bach's day, the sharp sign was made by a single or double cross symbol.) And in *Weinen, Klagen, Sorgen, Zagen*, cantata BWV 12, it will be found that in the middle of the opening choral movement, "At the sign of God," Bach constructs the melody in such a fashion that if the notes on the page are literally connected, as in the child's game "connect the dots," there is formed a series of crosses. This is taken a step further in the opening chorus of the *St. John Passion*, where the woodwinds above the turmoil depicted in the strings may be seen to form a series of crosses lying on their sides; the top layer of the entire opening chorus of the *St. John Passion* in a certain sense is a vivid pictorial image of crosses lying on the page of a conductor's score.

A slightly idiosyncratic example of *Augenmusik*, but one I hope not too far afield, is the aria from the *St. Matthew Passion*, "Komm, süsses Kreuz," for solo bass voice and viola da gamba obligato. I believe that Bach is making a double entendre here because the words are expressing on the one hand "Come, sweet cross, I will take you on, I will bear all of your burden," while on the other the gamba part is fantastically difficult from a technical standpoint: as the gamba visually forms a kind of cross by the strings and the bow, my view is that Bach is making a statement about the challenge of mastering this particular piece—along with its textual message—almost as if to say "I *will* master you, the music will become easy for me." It is really a statement about art and the responsibility of the artist.

I move now to what I call tonal symbolism, a symbolism that is more easily detected in that it is perceived with little effort by the listener if one follows the text and is aware of the individual words at any given moment. In the *St. Matthew Passion,* every time the word "betray" is declaimed by the Evangelist, Bach musically depicts it by a diminished or an augmented chord, which, as we know in music, "betrays" the harmony. In the same work, when the text deals with the message that "the flesh is willing but the spirit is weak," Bach sets the word "weak" on a diminished chord, a weak harmony, an unresolved harmony, one leading to a cadence. We hear teardrops in the first alto aria in the *St. Matthew Passion,* "Buss und Reu." We hear the teardrops plainly in the flute line with the staccato figures. We hear drops of blood in the soprano aria, "Blute nur" from the *St. Matthew Passion* when the text reads "Bleed on, dear heart." In the *B Minor Mass* we hear in the "Cruci-fixus" the drops of blood between the staccato notes very slowly in the flute line and the violins.

Yet another form of symbolism is suggested, for example, by the Evangelist's recitative in the *St. Matthew Passion* when he talks about the sheep being scattered, a point mirrored by the orchestra: the contrabasses and cellos descend while the violins and violas ascend. When the Evangelist talks of the ascension, we hear the orchestra strings playing a rising theme. Examples such as these are immediately obvious.

For a more veiled form of symbolism let us turn to the *St. Matthew Passion* once more. The center chorale of the work, "O Haupt voll Blut und Wunden" ("O head, full of blood and wounds"), the famous Passion Chorale is employed five times during the work, each time a half step lower except for the very last time. However, we are certainly not aware of hearing the same chorale four more times in the continuo line of four arias: for example the bass aria "Gerne" wherein the violin line takes our attention away from the continuo part sounding out the chorale tune. Or the tenor aria "Geduld" from the second part of the *Passion* where the lilting solo cello again distracts us from the fact that if we start on the second bar and isolate the first and third beats, we find it spelling out the chorale theme. In the alto aria "Erbarme dich," while we are taken by the intricate violin obligato, we are not conscious that in the bass "O Haupt" is being slowly stretched out underneath, or that in "Komm, süsses Kreuz" the initial note of the bar in the gamba part sketches out the same chorale.

As I previously mentioned, the motet *Jesus, meine Freude* is

concerned with the number 77 within the two symmetrical sections
of the motet, adding up to seven and seven, and seven and seven, as
well as the melody *B A C H* when the text proclaims "I will call thee
by name." Bach does this again, yet in reverse order in the aria
"Gerne" (*St. Matthew Passion*) at the point the bass sings "I drink
as my Saviour did" there ensues an orchestral ritornello based on
the notes "H" "C" "A" "B", Bach's name spelled backwards. Still
from the *St. Matthew Passion* we find that the music for the false
witnesses is set in canon, a most subtle way for the composer to tell
us that the false witnesses have concocted their stories before their
audience with Pontius Pilate, in that a canon cannot be improvised.

Other kinds of tonal symbolism we hear even more easily. At the
moment Peter says "Ich kenne des Menschen nicht" ("I know not
the man"), in the second part of the *St. Matthew Passion,* Bach
employs two levels of symbolism. First, he sets the tenor line with
the continuo in parallel fifths, the biggest transgression in music, as
any first-year student of harmony readily knows. Following this, the
Evangelist says "And immediately the cock crew." Now, looking at
the music on the page only, if you disregard momentarily that the
tenor part is notated in tenor clef, it will be observed that he sings
the exact notes as the bass (they will sound, of course, a fifth higher).
In this sense we have a combination of both sound and eye symbolism working simultaneously. Another example is in the aria following the scene where Judas hangs himself, "Gebt mir meinen Jesum
wieder" ("Give me back my Jesus"). What we hear in the solo violin
part is a series of rapid-fire 32nd notes, as the 30 pieces of silver are
flung across the floor. This is much the same as the famous dice-
rolling chorus from the *St John Passion,* "Lasset uns den nicht
zerteilen," where the soldiers cast for Jesus' robe. In the continuo,
with its quick-paced 16th notes, we actually hear the shaking of the
dice to which the chorus joins in as well on the word "losen" as the
notes literally spill out over the score.

As an aspect of symbolism, syncopation also plays a large role, and
a particularly fascinating one in Bach's tonal symbolism. Syncopation happens far too often in Bach's scores, especially in the *St.
Matthew Passion,* for one to disallow its presence. A graphic example of this may be seen at the moments Jesus steps outside of
humanity and becomes immortal; in essence, he is out of step with
his own time, "syncopated." And for me, as a performer and conductor, this has solved rather wonderfully things that before just seemed
mildly strange. In the chorale which stands as the centerpiece of
part two of the *Christmas Oratorio,* where the chorus sings of

Christ's birth—"Lo, here in this yonder stall lies the King and ruler of us all"—in the final line, the basses of the chorus all sing in syncopation, one note off from the rest of the chorus, as if to reinforce that the son of God is not to be a part of the human race. This can be observed in the *St. Matthew Passion* when the crowd says "His blood is on us and our children," and all are singing the main theme in syncopation, as if to signify this man is out of step with us.

Other manifestations of symbolism in the *St. Matthew Passion* appear to underlie an overall structure Bach was striving for. The Jews refer to the law of the Ten Commandments in ten choruses, that is, if we leave out the choruses sung by the Roman soldiers. We find three arias, not preceded by recitatives. Why is this? Because in these three arias they are prepared by the Evangelist talking about betrayal. And so Bach "betrays" us, the listener, by not setting the standard recitative plus aria formula. We find the chorus "Herr, bin ich" eleven bars long, the disciples asking "Lord is it I?" eleven times in all—the point being that all twelve disciples except Judas ask the question. In the eighth recitative,* it may be noted that the twelfth bar foretells of the coming of a new religion while at the same time telling the twelve disciples that this will take place. And in recitative eleven we find 30 notes for the Evangelist to sing as he relates how Jesus will be sold for 30 pieces of silver. Later, in the second part of the *Passion,* when Jesus is actually sold, at the moment the high priests count the 30 pieces of silver there are 30 notes in the continuo until they go on and say "This is the price we paid for His blood."

For me, the most important type of symbolism in Bach's music concerns those moments where there occurs a Biblical setting at the same time setting up things musically by numbers, the result being that there is yet another set of scripture, so to speak. In the *St. Matthew Passion* (during the Last Supper), we find in the only arioso Jesus sings Bach working on three layers of numerological significance simultaneously. As Jesus begins the Communion—"Take, this is my body"—from this point to the end of the recitative we find 365 pitches in the orchestra, suggesting the days of the year: a reference to the scriptural prophecy "I will be with you until the end of the world." When the Evangelist proclaims "And he took the cup, and gave thanks," Jesus responds with "Drink ye all of it, for this is my blood of the New Testament." From this point we find 116 notes in the bass; and Psalm 116 (in the Luther translation) is the only one of the Psalms to deal with the word "cup." When the Evangelist continues, "But I say unto you, henceforth no more will I

*I am using the old (BWV) numbering of movements.

drink this fruit of the vine, no more will I drink it until on that day," we discover 43 notes, those 43 notes being the day from Maundy Thursday to the ascension mentioned above as constituting the basis of the Christian's Credo.

In the recitative that launches the tenor aria "Geduld" the singer informs us Jesus "holds his peace" when the witnesses speak out against him. In Psalm 39, verse 10, in Luther's translation—it is important to note Luther's translation because the King James version is Psalm 39, verse 9—the text reads "I am dumb, I will not open my mouth because it is thy doing." And in the recitative there are exactly 39 notes in ten bars, undeniably a reference to Psalm 39, verse 10. Yet another example of this is to be found in the wonderfully effective earthquake scene so tellingly rendered by the rumble of the cellos that we forget to look at the page and find the cellos are playing a series of three sets of 32nd notes, the first totally 18 individual notes, the second 68 notes, and the third 104 notes. The three Psalms that speak of earthquakes are, not surprisingly, numbers 18, 68, and 104.

Of course such a topic as the one I have been addressing has in a certain sense no real conclusion in that one could clearly spend a lifetime discovering yet additional examples of all the above, and doubtless different categories in which to place examples. Nevertheless, allow me to conclude with the observation, no secret to many perhaps, only recently drawn to my attention by James Parsons, concerning the "Six Chorale Melodies" (BWV 645-650), the so-called *Schübler Chorales*. Although it has long been contended that the complete set was published ca. 1748-49, a much more convincing and plausible date, in view of Bach's passion for number symbolism and the lengths to which he went to depict this in his music, is the year 1750—the year in which Bach reached the age of 65. For me there can be no accident that the original title page bore exactly 65 words. Can the year of publication then really be any other but 1750?

The Articulation of Genre in Bach's Instrumental Music

Laurence Dreyfus

hen twentieth-century music historians treat the music of J. S. Bach, they inevitably turn to a discussion of his style. I think it is worthwhile to take a closer look at this term. What does it actually mean? If, by Bach's style, we merely mean the way Bach composed his music, is there anything in his music that is *not* stylistic? The question is far from frivolous. Consider the domains covered by the word style. There are the styles of genres, of epochs, of textures, of nations, institutions, instruments, and performance practices, not to mention the styles of individual composers. It is easy to cite well-entrenched usages within musicology: the sonata style, the Baroque style, homophonic style, French style, church style, organ style, authentic style, quite apart from Telemann's, Handel's or Bach's style. And furthermore, if we include in an individual composer's style all conceivable components of composition, the term threatens to crumble before our very eyes. Used to indicate everything and exclude nothing, style becomes too broad to explain very much at all.

Historically, of course—even in Bach's day—the term "style" signified a wide variety of things, including even the notion of an individual composer's style. Nonetheless, there is a subtle but crucial difference between historical and contemporary usage. Whereas style traditionally meant the manner by which a particular subject was expressed, style in musicology indicates a descriptive composite of all possible musical details. To put it another way: Style in traditional theory was assigned a value—high, middle, low, proper, improper, good, bad, bombastic, natural—while style in twentieth-century musical scholarship aspires to be value-free. This shift in meaning has had enormous consequences for the historiography and criticism of music. One of these consequences can be understood in the following way. By permitting style to embrace all sectors of musical description, we lose sight of a rich sector of traditional criticism which treated style as subordinate to genre. That is, a musical kind such as an aria, a fugue, a sonata, or a concerto represents a larger category than the style in which a particular piece is clothed. The present essay explores this straightforward point: namely, that we miss much of the historical specificity of Bach—those aspects which so distinguish him from his contemporaries—when we inflate the meaning of style and ignore the significance of genre.

The assumption that genre preceded style was often taken for granted in traditional criticism and sometimes went unmentioned. In 1589, for example, when the Elizabethan critic, George Puttenham, discussed examples of bad style, he noted that a style is indecorous when applied to the wrong subject. Aeneas, he wrote, should not *trudge* out of Troy nor should Juno *tug* Aeneas, for these terms are "better spoken of a beggar or of a rogue or a lackey."[1] His point on style presupposes a genre. Since, in the genre called epic, the hero is a personage of high station, the low style is inappropriate.[2]

In the German music theory of Bach's day, the explicit relation between musical genre or kind of style surfaces only infrequently, in part, because critics lacked a distinct word for genre or kind.[3] In fact, when discussing the matter abstractly, theorists used the word "style" to denote musical kinds (theater style or overture style), while when talking concretely they used the word "piece." Nonetheless one can infer the presupposition of genre in most discussions of style.[4] Consider in this regard Johann Mattheson writing on "musical style" in *Der vollkommene Kapellmeister* (1739). Citing examples of misapplied styles, he names such theatrical incongruities as 'beggars in a spirited minuet, slaves in a happy rigaudon, cowards in an heroic entree, despair in a lusty gavotte, or base spirits in a magnificent chaconne."[5] Or consider Johann Adolph Scheibe, Bach's famous detractor, writing in the *Critischer Musikus*. In describing the two sections of the French overture, Scheibe notes that the grave first section must "elevate a noble liveliness, a serious, masculine and grandiose manner"[6] thereby enumerating the qualities by which he elsewhere described the high style.[7] The second section, on the other hand, a fugue, must be "free, lively and sometimes even playful,"[8] that is, in middle style.[9] Style, therefore, implicates a genre as soon as Scheibe talks about an actual piece of music. Moreover, in

concrete discussions, the musical kind precedes the mention of
the appropriate style. First, Scheibe says that the second part of
an overture is a fugue, and then he recommends an appropriate
middle-style.[10]

The implicit relation between genre and style also suggests that,
with a modern musicological notion of style, Scheibe's attack against
Bach has been misunderstood. When Scheibe criticized Bach for
bombast and confusion and recommended more "agreeableness,"
he was not censuring Bach's style in our modern sense. Instead he
condemned Bach's overly wrought application of high style.[11] For
example, in explaining the so-called "bombastic style," a deforma-
tion of high style, Scheibe repeats the very same objections raised in
his previous attack, making it clear that he was thinking of none
other than J. S. Bach:

> These are the leading characteristics of the bombastic style,
> with which even great masters of music have fallen in love,
> [those] who otherwise could give us the most excellent models
> of a good or even truly high style if they would join reasonable
> judgment to their skill and knowledge of music and follow
> nature rather than art.[12]

This is why Scheibe, elsewhere in the *Critischer Musikus*, can
single out Bach—among Hasse, Graun and Telemann—as a particular master of metaphorical or "florid expression"[13] or how he can
praise Bach, together with Handel, for keyboard music exemplifying
a consummate arrangement, decoration and elaboration.[14] Instead of
censuring Bach's style across the board in the sense of technical
aggregate, Scheibe is saying that, in those genres, vocal or instrumental, in which the high style is appropriate, Bach has a mistaken
notion of taste and has been misled by artifice.

Yet another problem with our modern notion of Bach's style is
that it presumes a singular manner of expression regardless of genre.
Common sense alone tells us that the styles appropriate to a cantata
aria differ measurably from those appropriate to an Allemande or a
canon, yet we persist in speaking of Bach's style as if it were
something tangible, a composite of features that can decide questions of authenticity or determine a chronology. Take, for example,
the discussions doubting the authenticity of Bach's famous D-minor
harpsichord concerto (BWV 1052), which have appealed precisely
to such a unitary notion of Bach's style. Hans-Joachim Schulze's
views are typical in this regard. The form and character of the
thematic subjects, the lack of true concertante writing, the frequent

unison writing in the ripieno violins, among other stylistic criteria, make it doubtful that the original work was in all its parts a creation of J.S. Bach.[15] What Schulze neglects is a consideration of both the range of stylistic devices conceivable in a Bach concerto and, more importantly, the highly individual profiles of Bach's concerto *oeuvre*. In the first case, the character of the thematic subject conforms not to some notion of Bach's style, but to a certain *type* of Bach concerto, namely the kind with a unison ritornello. In the second case, the apparently Italianate simplicity coincides with formal manipulations of the genre which no one beside Bach seems to have engaged in. Style considered apart from genre therefore runs the risk of demanding a standard for consistency which forgets the difference between, if you will, apples and oranges.

Modern notions of musical style have also confused issues of chronology. An example is the 6th Brandenburg concerto. Here the stylistic aspects of the first movement—five part texture, canonic writing, the absence of violins, the use of viola da gambas, the lack of a Vivaldian subject—all suggest an early dating for the work. This idea assumes that Bach began writing concertos in a more old-fashioned style and then progressed to more up-to-date procedures. Yet this view ignores the features of genre in the 6th Brandenburg, which are far from old-fashioned. Earlier works from the late seventeenth century by Krieger, Rosenmüller, or Erlebach, for example, employing apparently similar styles bear no resemblance to the formal processes attached to Bach's concertos with Vivaldian ritornellos. Moreover, even the one Weimar Sinfonia to Cantata 18, which the instrumentation of the 6th Brandenburg recalls, reflects a different kind of concerto, the type with a unison ritornello subject, which is based on another set of formal operations. People, it seems necessary to state, do not live lives encased in a style. Rather, people use styles to lend shape and meaning to basic kinds of experiences.

On the preceding pages, I have attempted to cast aspersions on the usual notions of musical style—in an admittedly somewhat exaggerated fashion—so as to indicate at least some of the havoc wreaked by this all-embracing concept. Having done so, I need to propose some alternative. It runs something like this: Style does not signify everything in music but rather highlights some supplemental way of expressing a genre. One cannot replace the words "style" or "stylistic" with the words "music" or "musical." It follows that styles can have varied attitudes toward musical kinds.

Styles, for example, can fit snugly with genres. A minuet with alternating quarters and eighths containing few dissonances and the barest of ornaments furnishes a good example of a snug fit. Here the style is so proper to the dance that, by avoiding other generic references or high-style designs, it meshes in seamlessly with the semantic fabric of the minuet.

Styles can also lend a special identity to a genre by imparting a specific meaning congruent with the kind's values. For example, the fugue in the second part of a French overture leans toward the playful while the fugue proper to a Kyrie or Gloria more appropriately entails invertible counterpoint, canons and double fugues.[16] In each case, the genre takes on a specific profile because of the style in which it is cast.

Finally, styles can conflict with genres. That is, just like the error of Aeneas trudging out of Troy, where a beggarly verb compromises an epic hero, style in music can clash with a genre. A learned chromatic minuet or a pastoral Kyrie would furnish two such examples according to the implicit standards of Bach's day. Yet Bach, in common with other masters of music, painting and literature, can be accused of precisely such apparent abuses. It is noteworthy of course that Bach's tendency most often is to uplift genres by employing a style ordinarily considered too high. Perhaps, in keeping with his theological belief regarding the divine character of music, Bach leaned towards what can be termed generic elevation, in which any musical kind can be dignified with the noble aspirations of the high style. At the same time, with a different purpose in mind, he also expressed elevated genres, as we shall see, with styles from the middle range. While the subject of discontinuity between genre and style requires further exploration, suffice it to say that the conflict is not minimized merely because the best composers engaged in it. On the contrary, the individuality of a work embodying such a conflict depends precisely on the disagreement between genre and style.

What then is a genre? Put most simply, it is one of the kinds of music which people conversant in a culture name with a noun.[17] They say: This is a canon, a fugue, an aria, a recitative, a sonata, a sarabande, a chorale. When these same people become more specific and mention a trio sonata, a grave sarabande or an accompanied recitative, or a simple chorale setting, they name subsidiary types of a genre, that is, more restrictive versions of the basic kinds. On the other hand, when they refer to kinds via adjectives, such as canonic, fugal, concerted, recitative-like, they are no longer referring to the genre itself but rather to its mode. One says: a fugal gigue movement, an aria-like sonata slow movement, a canonic variation, a trio concertante or an aria in the manner of a passepied. That is, a generic mode dispenses with the characteristic size and formal scheme of a genre and merely reproduces certain of its repertoire of possible features. Even more than style, the generic mode constitutes an important tool by which musical works take on singular identities. Genres, finally, have characteristic forms—arias are *da capo*, minuets are binary with four bar-phrases, fugues begin with imitation at the fifth, concertos alternate between ritornellos and solo episodes. But to talk about characteristic forms does not imply a predictive chronological plan for each event of a musical work. On the contrary, the notion of a quasi-narrative form we associate with the Viennese Classical sonata is simply not operative in most musical genres. Form need not imply a particular sequence of events but merely the significant operations and shapes which help to identify the genre. Like style, form is a characteristic of genre.

✿   ✿   ✿   ✿   ✿

To explore the special relation in Bach's works between genre, mode and style, I turn first to a seemingly modest work from the *Clavierübung,* Part II, called "Echo" which concludes the B-minor Overture. (This movement is given in its entirety in Example 1a.)

Since the outward size, shape and even style of this unassuming character piece signal the genre of the *galanterie,* it is easy to mistake the complexities of the "Echo." Philipp Spitta, for example, saw in it only "a dance from which exhibits no definite type."[18] As for a critical evaluation of the piece, he found the echo effects "especially charming because the phrases are not repeated exactly." Yet Spitta also expressed some disappointment with the "Echo," noting that here, as in other movements comprising the *French Overtüre,* there remains "a popular character not proper to real keyboard partitas."[19]

What Spitta missed lay behind the playful stylistic exterior. For despite the surface *galanterie,* the generic mode of the "Echo" is severely concerto-like, representing nothing less than a catalog of Bach's ritornello procedures. One might even coin the term *Galanteriestück auf Concertenart*—a galant character piece in the mode of a concerto—to capture the extraordinary world inhabited by the "Echo." To grasp the fascinating relation between generic foreground and modal background, the inner workings of the "Echo" need to be explored in some detail.

To say that Bach casts the "Echo" in the generic mode of a concerto does not only mean that the *forte* and *piano* markings

R1
S1
piano
forte
piano
forte
R2
piano
forte
forte
S2
piano
forte

Example 1a

piano
R3
forte
28
piano
forte
piano
forte
1.
2.
R4
R5
36
S3
piano
forte
piano
forte
40
R6
piano
44

Example 1a

R7
53
S4
piano
forte
piano
58
forte
piano
forte
R8
piano
forte
62
66
68
piano
forte
piano
forte
Fine

Example 1a

signal the tutti and solo forces in the concerto grosso. Unlike his contemporaries, Bach early on had consigned the tutti-solo distinction to the decoration of the work rather than its invention. Instead, what motivates Bach's concerto *ocuvre* is a more abstract principle—the presence, absence and recasting of a ritornello. Far from an identity determined merely by asking who is playing it, Bach's ritornellos have shapes determined by regular harmonic conventions.

Wilhelm Fischer, a music historian writing some seventy years ago, coined the terms *Vordersatz, Fortspinnung* and *Epilog* to identify the three segments of a concerto ritornello.[20] In so doing, he insightfully captured the organization of the leading subsidiary kind among Bach's concertos. But whereas Fischer emphasized the melodic and motivic characteristics of the ritornello, it is easily shown that the segments actually display a more regular harmonic profile, in which each contributes to a complete, tonally closed invention. One can easily hear this profile in the ritornello to Bach's E-major violin concerto, BWV 1042, even without the score in hand. The *Vordersatz* ([V]) defines the tonic chord by reference to its dominant. *How* it accomplishes this—broken arpeggios, scale figures, a succession of short motives—is therefore subordinate to *whether* it does so by clearly evident triads in root position moving from the tonic to the dominant. The *Fortspinnung* ([F]), on the other hand, is based on the absence of either a defined tonic or an authentic cadence resolving the tonic. It therefore displays either conventional voice-leading sequences (such as 10-7-10-7, 5-6-5-6 or 10-10-10) or more random contrapuntal motion. In any event, it delays, through linear means, a strong tonal articulation. The *Epilog* ([E]), on the other hand, presents the formal cadence in the tonic closing on the first scale step in the upper voice.[21] By contrast, the solo sections are identified not so much by contrasting "themes" as by the absence of ritornello segments. Understood in this way, Bach's concertos stand apart from the narrative, chronological form important to the later Viennese sonata. The number of ritornellos, the order of the tonal stations, the motivic relations between tutti and solo themes are therefore not really structural issues of this genre. Neither are Bach's works molded in a concerto form, which would predict the order and significance of events. Instead, a Bach concerto is structured primarily on a set of formal operations performed on an "ideal ritornello" which underlies a particular work.

A glance at the voice-leading underlying the proposed ideal ritornello for the "Echo" in Example 1b reveals a remarkably regular

Example 1b

segmentation. Both segments of the *Vordersatz*, as can be seen, independently establish the tonic. The *Fortspinnung*, beginning with a usual intervallic succession, withholds a definition or resolution of the tonic and sets up the typical move to the dominant seventh. The *Epilog*, takes a conventional route to the cadence. Here is the ideal ritornello heard with its segments linked together. The ritornello segments, moreover, stand out in bold relief when compared to the voice-leading of the solo episodes. Consider Example 1c. As the example shows, the solo episodes neither reproduce the ritornello functions nor, for that matter, even repeat themselves, this despite the outward motivic unity they display. This lack of structural repetition is one reason why S1 in mm. 5ff cannot form a *Fortspinnung*. Moreover, it cannot link up with a cadential *Epilog* segment. Interestingly, the charming echo effects which prompted Spitta's stylistic analysis occur in these solo episodes—S_2 and S_4. Unlike the strict reformulations found in the ritornello segmentation, these passages play no role in structuring the piece as a whole, although they support the generic identification of the piece as a *galanterie*.

What I find so fascinating about this movement is that, despite its apparent genre—with its binary form and its ostensibly *galant* manners, the "Echo" manages to display virtually every ritornello func-

Example 1c

tion as rigorously as any Bach concerto one could cite. Through the grid of ritornello occurrences represented in Table 1, the work establishes its concerto-like credentials.

First, the ritornello can be said to SEGMENT, which is to say that the ritornello displays its functional subdivisions. The appearance of a partial ritornello, moreover, entails certain logical consequences. For example, R_3 beginning in m. 26 presents only the *Fortspinnung* and *Epilog*, thus functioning as a resolution to the preceding material. Indeed, this confers a pseudo-*Vordersatz*-like status on the previous solo episode, S_2, beginning in bar 22. Note, however, that S_2 can never replace the real *Vordersatz* because it lacks a dominant chord which would have defined the tonic.

Next, the ritornello can be said to DECORATE. This term signifies the processes that alter surface identities but adhere to the underlying harmonic structure. Examples of this function abound in the "Echo." Consider, for instance, the final statement of the *Vordersatz* in m. 62. Here the intervallic inversion of the voices causes the ritornello "subject" to migrate to the tenor part over an ornamental dominant pedal. The change is DECORATive rather than structural, since the shape of the piece would not change if we substituted the earlier version of the *Vordersatz* for this DECORATed one. Similarly, metric and rhythmic variants also play a role in this function. Consider next the DECORATed *Epilog* of R_2 in mm. 20-22 compared with the ideal *Epilog* postulated in Example 1b. Here the four-

Table 1
Ritornello Formations in the "Echo"

Ritornello	Key	Mode	Measures	Segments
R_1	I	minor	1-4	$[V_1 \ V_2]$
R_2	V	minor	13-22	$[V_1 \ V_2 \cdot F - E^\bullet]$
R_3	V	minor	26-32	$[F - E^\bullet]$
R_4	III	MAJOR	33-34	$[V_1 \ V_2]$
R_5	IV	minor	35-36	
R_6	VI	MAJOR	45-48	$[V_1 \ V_2 \cdot F - E^\bullet]$
R_7	IV	minor	49-54	
R_8	I	minor	62-72	$[V_1 \cdot \ V_2 \ F - E]$

bar length in the ideal ritornello is compressed into three bars in R_2 without altering the voice-leading. In each case of DECORATion one can always substitute the ideal form for the surface variant to test for their grammatical equivalence. By these subtle semantic shifts, Bach's concertos are able to dramatize the opposition between surface features and the deeper tonal order.

In a special form of the function DECORATE I call OR-CHESTRATE, the composer deploys *piano* and *forte* markings so as to signify tutti/solo distinctions which imaginatively mask the underlying polarity between ritornello and (solo) episode. The "Echo" includes a plethora of such markings. Sometimes the composer ORCHESTRATEs solo sections as "tuttis," such as in the *forte* markings in mm. 5 through 12. At other times, however, he ORCHESTRATEs a ritornello segment as a "solo setting" as in mm. 13 through 16 when the *Vordersatz* of R_2 is marked *piano*.

The ritornellos in the "Echo" also display a wide ARRAY of segments transposed into significant keys, here presenting segments in five different tonal regions as shown in Table 1 under the column labeled "Key." The sequential order of the ARRAYed key areas is, of course, far from haphazard and reflects the usual hierarchy of scale steps. However, it is revealing to stress the essential lack of a preordained harmonic plan for each transposition of the tonal ARRAY.

Related to the ARRAY is an important process called MODE-SWITCH, which translates major ritornellos into the minor and minor ritornellos into the major. MODESWITCH then checks for syntactic errors and rejects segments it has rendered ungrammatical. Here, as Table 1 shows, the *Vordersatz* segments lend themselves to modal translation and are so used in R_4 and R_6. Translation of the *Fortspinnung* into the major, on the other hand, caused an incorrect doubling in a diminished chord, a voice-leading error which rendered it unusable.

In a more subtle process, the ritornello principle in the "Echo" also RESEARCHes hidden relations between segments already transposed by the ARRAY and translated by MODESWITCH. This occurs in R_4 and R_5 as well as in R_6 and R_7. Consider R_6 and R_7 in bars 45 through 54. At first glance, this passage seems to comprise a modulating ritornello, that is, an ungrammatical departure dictated by a new harmonic goal. Upon closer inspection, however, the fourteen measures reveal that Bach has coupled two ritornello segments ARRAYed in different keys. The coupling is far from accidental but proceeds from a felicitous coincidence of voice-leading at the end of [V_2] in bar 48. Consider here Example 1d. As the reduction

MODESWITCH [V₁₋₂]
ARRAY [V₁₋₂] in VI

DECORATE [V₂]=[V₂*]   ARRAY [F-E*] in VI

Example 1d

shows, the *Vordersatz* in G major connects seamlessly to the *Fortspinnung* in E minor through a stepwise ascent between the two tenths. The RESEARCH which looks for the compatibility of unusual segmentations also works hand in hand with MODESWITCH: After rejecting an ungrammatical *Fortspinnung* in major, Bach RESEARCHed an alternative link to a permissible *Fortspinnung* in minor. He found it by coupling the *Vordersatz* in the submediant to the *Fortspinnung* in the subdominant.

The staggering ingenuity of the "Echo" embraces several ironies. Chief among these is that it represents a much better *Bach* concerto than does the first movement of the Italian Concerto which opens the *Clavierübung*, Part II. This latter movement, despite its size and form indicating a real concerto movement, does not exploit the ritornello segments as do Bach's most advanced works in this genre. For example, as Table 2 shows, the ritornello formations in this

TABLE 2
Ritornello Formations in BWV 971/1
(Italian Concerto, movement 1)

Ritornello	Key	Mode	Measures	Segments
R_1	I	MAJOR	1-30	V F E
R_2	VI	minor	73-90	E
R_3	I	MAJOR	163-192	V F E

movement of the Italian Concerto are strikingly more primitive than
those of the "Echo." With its two identical framing ritornellos, the
piece seems positively disinterested in exploring the substance and
sense of its segmentation. Thus, while the "Echo" owes a generic
allegiance to the *galanterie*, a light binary piece at the end of a suite,
its concerted mode challenges a simple identification and brings it
face to face with an inappropriately more involved and intricate
genre. It can therefore be distinguished both from the Badinerie in
the B-minor orchestral suite, a true galant character piece, as well as
from the "Prelude" to the E-major partita for violin, a mock concerted work playing merely on dynamic contrast. The style of the
"Echo" is therefore highly paradoxical. To the extent one recognizes
the concerto structure it must be pronounced relatively high; to the
extent one hears the hedonistic galant tone of the echo elements, it
must be valued much lower. An analysis cannot really bring these
two divergent moments into a unified synthesis, but can merely
organize them hierarchically. The stricter generic mode of the concerto is certainly what pulls the strings if only because of the
physical space its operations occupy within the piece. What remains
clear is that both the power and appeal of this work depend on this
curious disjuncture between genre, mode and style.

✻   ✻   ✻   ✻   ✻

As in the case of the "Echo," to talk coherently about the constella-
tion of ritornello segments, one could posit the ideal ritornello as a
starting point for the work. To put it more specifically: The "invention" of the work depends on an "ideal ritornello" which precedes
the work but need not be identified with its opening gesture. The
stylistic aspects of the "Echo"—especially its echo effects—could not
have generated the rigorous structure of the piece but had to be
painted, as it were, above the inventive work of the ritornello
principle.

The same applies even in a real Bach concerto, in which the
structural principles of the genre can be shown to outweigh both the
conventional formal layout as well as the stylistic features appropriate to its performing forces. To illustrate this point, we turn to the
first movement of the *Brandenburg Concerto No. 2*. Here the
specific kind of concerto—the group concerto with a concertino of
four solo instruments—does not organize more than the surface
details of the movement. Instead, the instruments either contribute
to the ORCHESTRATion of the ritornellos or else participate in

motivically clothed solo episodes whose linear movement leads to
the various appearances of the tonal ARRAY.

Although its opening ritornello (given in Example 2) seems,
through its familiarity, to epitomize Bach's concertos, there is really
something peculiar about it. If one slices up the opening 8 measures
in traditional terms, it is easy to isolate the four "balanced" phrases
that comprise the ritornello. But these are not, it turns out, the sort
of distinctive segments that generate ritornello movements elsewhere. The first two measures, for instance—we call them [V_a]—lack

Example 2

a confirming dominant. To function as a complete *Vordersatz*, they therefore require measures 3 and 4—let us call them [V_b]. The following measures contain nothing resembling a *Fortspinnung*, for immediately thereafter, at m. 5, the ritornello returns to the tonic and sets up the cadence in m. 8. Although grammatical enough in tonal terms, this ritornello clearly countermands the code characterizing other concerto-ritornello movements. What is striking, however, is the use Bach puts to the opening two measures. As you recall, the entrances of the four solo instruments immediately after the opening ritornello are punctuated by isolated statements of this [V_a] fragment. As a consequence, Bach manages to avoid the typically Vivaldian tonal redundancy so near the beginning of the piece while he satisfies the relatively superficial demands of the generic sub-type, the group concerto.

Nonetheless, as Table 3A shows, R_1 never again appears intact anywhere in the movement. On the contrary, Bach employs what seems to be a competing and more conventional ritornello configuration on three separate occasions. (One of these—R_7—is given in Example 3.) Here a clearly demarcated *Fortspinnung* substitutes for the fragment [V_b]. Even without an intimate familiarity with this Brandenburg concerto, one might probably agree that this ritornello, like the "ideal" ritornello in the "Echo," better approximates the conventional segmentation than does the opening ritornello. One interesting corollary of this later ritornello is that the *Epilog*—identical in both versions—only now makes good sense. Its emphasis on the tonic occurs after the withdrawal of the tonal center during the F-segment, whereas previously it had sounded redundant. On the other hand, this later ritornello has a defective *Vordersatz*. For by omitting the fragment [V_b], it is never able to confirm the tonic. To sum up: Neither ritornello formation is complete, though both exhibit complementary defects.

This relation surfaces in yet another way, since Bach sets the opening ritornello in major while he casts all the later ritornellos containing the *Fortspinnung* in minor. Table 3B tries to account for both the major and minor modes except for the *Fortspinnung*. Example 4 indicates how a MODESWITCH of the *Fortspinnung* would have doubled the root of the leading-tone chord in major. Indeed, Bach already exploits all possible permutations here except this impermissible one, going so far as to translate even [V_b] into the minor in R_6. But he cannot have it both ways. For the generating ideas that spark the movement refuse to congeal into a coherent structure. Given the systemic constraints which his own ideas

Example 3

Example 4

TABLE 3A
Ritornello Formations in BWV 1047/1
Brandenburg Concerto No. 2, Movement 1

Ritornello	Key	Mode	Measures	Segments				
R_1	I	MAJOR	1-8	V_a	V_b			E
R_2	V	MAJOR	23-28		V_b			E
R_3	VI	minor	31-39	V_a			F	E
R_4	I	MAJOR	46-49	V_a	V_b			
R_5	IV	MAJOR	56-59					E
R_6	V	minor	68-71	V_a	V_b			
R_7	II	minor	75-83	V_a			F	E
R_8	III	minor	94-102	V_a			F	E
R_9	I	MAJOR	103-106,	[V_a	V_b]			
			115-118					[E]

TABLE 3B
"MODE-SWITCH" COMPARISON

	MAJOR	minor
[V_a]	x	x
[V_b]	x	x
[F]	non-occurrent	x
[E]	x	x

accept, Bach cannot write a grammatical ritornello in major because it will lack a *Fortspinnung* as in Ritornello$_X$. (See the bottom of the Diagram.) But neither can he write a grammatical one in minor because the *Vordersatz* never establishes the tonic, as in Ritornello$_Y$.

We then face the inevitable, nagging question: Which came first? Let us imagine, for instance, that Bach first thought of the opening

DIAGRAM
THE "INVENTION" OF BWV 1047/1

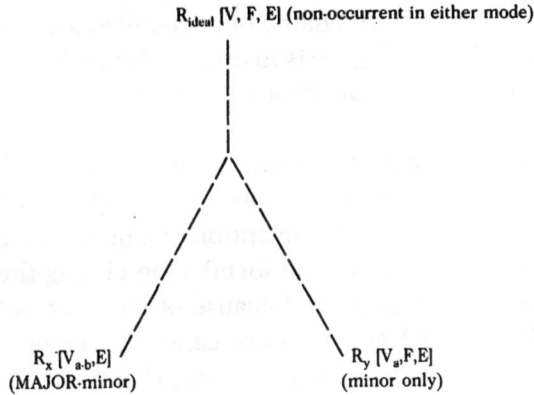

R_{ideal} [V, F, E] (non-occurrent in either mode)

R_x [$V_{a\text{-}b}$,E] R_y [V_a,F,E]
(MAJOR-minor)   (minor only)

Vordersatz. This would explain how he uses the initial fragment to introduce the soloists. However, this means that there was no way for him to conceive of a grammatical *Fortspinnung* and *Epilog* connected to the *Vordersatz*, which is, after all, what the invention of a *Vordersatz* automatically entails. Let us imagine, on the other hand, that Bach conceived the first *Vordersatz* fragment *together* with the two grammatical segments that follow. This would, to be sure, explain the raison d'être of the *Epilog*, which seems to follow naturally on the heels of a *Fortspinnung*. But that means that Bach would have had to conceive a minor ritornello for a piece in major— a scarcely imaginable possibility. Moreover, the incomplete *Vordersatz* in minor still lacks a stable tonic and can hardly have served as an initial ritornello. The diagram schematizes the process I have been describing in which, if you will, Bach thinks what is musically unthinkable. To put it another way: The subject of this utopian ritornello is a struggle between the free play of musical invention and the necessary dictates of the genre. Neither can win given the rules of the game, yet, happily for us, the *Second Brandenburg Concerto* represents the negotiated truce.

✻   ✻   ✻   ✻   ✻

The notion of style has caused particular confusion with the genre of fugue. To give a schematic overview, the nineteenth-century theorists invented a fugal form, largely to help students write academic fugues in music conservatories. Once the music historians started considering the matter seriously, they discovered that Bach did not write rigid forms for fugue. Fugue was then devalued into a style, or, at best, a pedagogical technique from which the great art-composer deviated in the name of poetic license. The best one could hope for with Bach's fugues is to arrange them descriptively by style: stile antico, instrumental idiom, canzona, dance subject, ricercare, and so on.[22]

But style does not determine genre in fugue. Rather, it again decorates the essential invention underlying the work in question. Where then is the essential invention of a fugue if the genre does not depend on style or discursive form? One clue is the generally high value assessed to this genre because of its compositional difficulty. Among the learned genres, only canon occupies a more coveted position. Indeed, one can say that, in principle, a fugue is valued to the extent that it aspires to the highest levels of artifice. Since the more demanding the fugue, the greater the amount of contrapuntal and imitative devices, it is revealing to rethink the genre in terms of its degree of strictness instead of plotting the pieces by chronological events or by identifying the style.

The first fugue in the *Well-Tempered Clavier* Book I proves most instructive from this vantage point. (The piece is given in Example 5.) Table 4 decomposes the contrapuntal structures of the piece by

Example 5

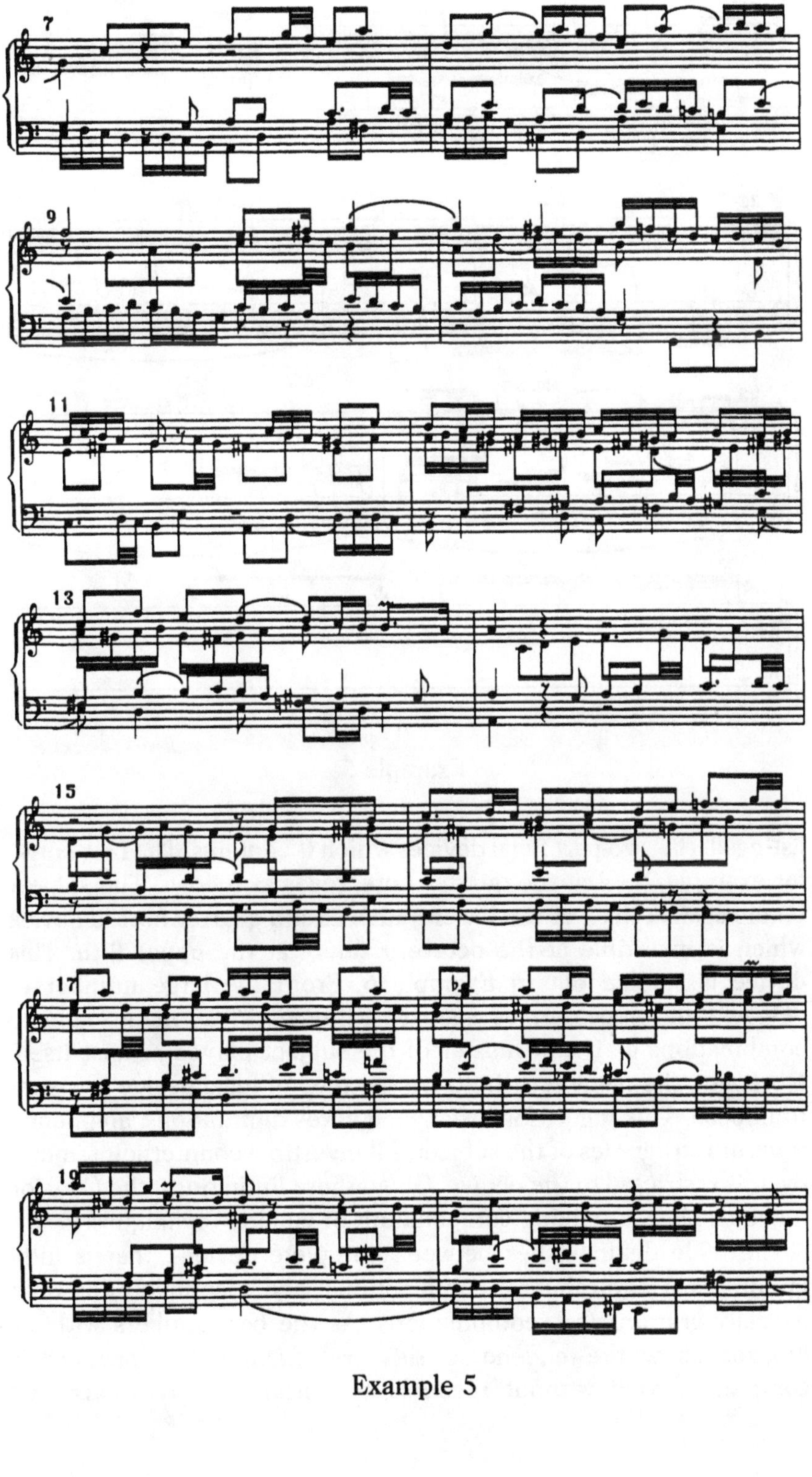

Example 5

Example 5

listing all the two-part fugal devices which it contains. The first entry, for example, S - 4 at the quarter note, reads as follows: The subject enters against itself at the lower fourth after a quarter note, a device which is invertible at the octave, namely at the upper fifth. This device is spelled out in Example 6. From the large number of devices, the piece can be seen to RESEARCH· as many canonic combinations as it can muster of the subject played against itself. Moreover, the piece sets limits on the type of fugal device it wishes to impose. This fugue, for instance, ignores diminutions, augmentations or retrogrades of the subject. All invertible counterpoint, moreover, is restricted to the octave. Given these limitations, the C-major fugue displays a striking compendium of generic techniques.

The table distinguishes between complete devices, that is fully grammatical contrapuntal combinations, and incomplete, or only partially grammatical, combinations. As the bar numbers without brackets show, the tendency of this strict fugue is to express each complete device without recourse to chromatic alterations. For

TABLE 4
Fugal Devices in WTC I/1

Complete devices	Device begins in bar:
1. ⌈ S – 4 (♩)	7, [14], 16
⌊ S + 5 (♩)	[10], [19], [24]
2. ⌈ S + 4 (♩)	24
⌊ S – 5 (♩)	[17]
3. S – 4 (○)	14, [16]
4. S – 3 (♩)	[17]
5. S + 4 (○♩)	15
6. S – 7 (○♩)	10, [16]
7. S – 8 (○♩)	[19]
Incomplete devices	
8. S – 7 (♩)	(16) altered
9. S + 8 (♩)	(15) aborted
10. S – 6 (♩)	(20) aborted
11. S + 3 (♩)	(20) aborted
12. ⌈ S – 8 (♩)	(14) aborted
⌊ S + 8 (♩)	(24) aborted

S   Subject
[ ]   position of altered or incomplete statement of a complete device
( )   position of altered or aborted ungrammatical devices

Example 6

example, Devices 1, 2, 3, 5 and 6 are all expressed at least once in an unaltered form. Device 4 could have been presented without alteration but is subordinated to Device 1 in a three-voice canonic complex. The complete devices are, in any case, hierarchical. The shorter the time span between imitations, the more difficult the combinations. That is, the greater the overlap, the more challenging the counterpoint. Bach therefore had to work out the subject while planning at least the combinations separated by quarters and half notes. At the other end of the spectrum—in imitations where the two parts overlap only briefly—the complete devices were perhaps no more than felicitous coincidences of voice-leading.

The incomplete devices reveal interesting evidence that Bach's fugues contain remnants of his work RESEARCHing the canonic possibilities of his subject. Two types of devices figure here: those which are aborted midway into the imitation and those which are altered and used whole. Consider here Device 12, imitation at the upper octave at the distance of a dotted half in Example 7. The unprepared fourth on the third overlapping eighth could easily be remedied by a free bass voice below. Unsalvageable, however, were the forbidden parallel octaves between the asterisked notes. Consider next bars 24-25. Significantly, Bach has used Device 12 until the very moment when it becomes ungrammatical. Indeed, in each instance of an aborted ungrammatical device in the C major fugue, Bach exploits the imitation until he is forced to stop. Instead of having designed these entrances informally to enhance the pile-up of voices—an interpretation suggested by the misleading term, false stretto[23]—Bach aborts a device because to have continued would have produced an error of voice-leading. One further aspect of the strict fugue, therefore, is its tendency to include as many as possible of the rejected versions which figured in the fugal RESEARCH.

In the case of altered devices, Bach makes small chromatic adjustments in order to salvage the imitative attempt, although, in the course of the fugue, the weight of the imitative work is borne by the

Example 7

complete devices. Such an example is Device 8, an imitation at the
lower seventh after a half note. Consider Example 8, in which Device
8 occurs between the alto and tenor voices. One reason this passage
is so fascinating is that a number of complete devices are heard
within one contrapuntal environment. Here the reigning imitation—
Device 1—occurs between soprano and alto and the alterations in
the tenor and bass accommodate the necessities of proper voice-
leading.

Example 8

Bach's attempt to record within the C-major fugue as many contrapuntal combinations as he could find means that independent harmonic progressions were severely circumscribed. Since he writes at
least two voices in imitation almost continuously from m. 7 to the
end, Bach used the non-canonic parts chiefly to enrich the linear
counterpoint. What is significant, although not surprising, is that the
points of tonal definition—and there are precious few—take place
outside the fugal work itself. That is, the harmonic articulation of the
strict fugue does not generally interact with the inventions which
structure the genre. While Bach can of course situate a fugal device
on a particular scale-step to indicate a harmonic goal or to chromatically alter a device so as to favor a harmonic direction, this is a far
cry from the genres—such as the concerto—where the harmonic
structure can be seen to pull the strings. Within the spectrum of
fugal kinds—one might say—harmonic control stands in inverse
proportion to the degree of contrapuntal severity.

If we now reinsert the devices into the chronological sequence of the piece, several features of the genre call for comment. First, the beginning of the fugue seems a positively lax affair, since the subject is merely introduced in all four parts but without any fugal devices. The so-called fugal exposition figures therefore chiefly as an indicator of genre: With this opening Bach assures us that he is writing a fugue. On the other hand, the opening need not reveal what this particular fugue will entail. The *style* of the subject likewise has little influence on the range of devices which a fugue will explore. Here the agreeable instrumental style, avoiding the stern face of the vocal *stile antico*, does not really suit the severe generic drama which will unfold later in the piece. Indeed, the casual atmosphere of the opening belies the artifice with which the work is crafted. In one sense, Bach should more appropriately have cast the work in a higher style. On the other hand, this stylistic orientation endows the work with a value traditionally cherished in fugue: the sense of *creatio ex nihilo*. For the style counterpoints a move from the simple two-part devices in mm. 7 and 10 to the complex three-and four-part devices which fill the second half of the fugue, although not in any predictable sequence. In this way, the drama of the genre can be seen as an ever more astonishing multiplication of devices, which, although they begin simply and progressively become more arcane, cannot have been conceived in the same order.

☼   ☼   ☼   ☼   ☼

One can therefore take two attitudes towards style. Either style is organic or it is additive.[24] The organic notion is tantamount to the dictum that "le style est l'homme même" (Buffon) or "style makes the man." This view might be seen to rely on the truism that there is no content without expression, no thought without language, no genre without style. Yet the very linguistic distinction we draw between kind and style intuitively points up some meaningful semantic distinction. It is not so much a problem which can be settled by an appeal to logic but, given its nature, must be elucidated by the human beings who depend on the difference. In musical scholarship, it goes without saying that the realm of style analysis has had a certain degree of success in distinguishing composers, particularly great composers, from their contemporaries, sometimes even producing a multi-dimensional criticism filled with penetrating insights. Yet I think one could make the case that the best practitioners of style analysis were already practicing what one might call genre criticism. That is, rather than producing positive composites of the styles of Mozart, Beethoven or Stravinsky, writers have perhaps captured most when explaining Mozart's concertos, Beethoven's string quartets or Stravinsky's ballets.

In the preceding discussion of a few of Bach's instrumental works, I have hoped to show that an individual work proves more revealing when it is read within and against the genres and styles which constitute it. I think it is also fair to say that the relation between genre and style is not merely a matter for contemporary criticism but was also an issue for Bach himself. No other composer of his day indulged in such a life-long exercise in rethinking the fundamental principles of the genres, working through their nexus of relations and reformulating the possible styles in which they could be expressed. It is this multitude of processes and not the myth of a unitary style which accounts in large part, I think, for the enormous gulf which separates Bach from his contemporaries. If Bach achieved more than his contemporaries, it was precisely because he refused to succumb to a facile determination of style. Indeed, it was during his lifetime that critics such as Scheibe and Mattheson began to conceive of a higher tribunal for style—namely the court of fashion, which, in the name of naturalness (*das Natürliche*) fostered a decline in the ability of music to speculate both on itself and on the world. New genres of course came into being under the fashionable slogans. And a new generation of Bach devotees such as Marpurg and Kirnberger began the complicated task of assessing his accomplishments. But neither the tastefulness of the new genres nor the advances in music theory compensated for the loss of a historical moment in which a great musical mind—somewhat removed from mainstream successes—reflected on the totality of musical kinds with an ingenuity that forever altered the sense and meaning of the individual musical work.

Notes

1. George Puttenham, *The Art of English Poesy*, cited in Laurence D. Lerner, "Style," *Princeton Encyclopedia of Poetry and Poetics* (Princeton, 1974), 815.

2. Earlier, Puttenham is explicit that styles suit genres, high for epic and tragedy, the middle for common love poems and elegies, and the base for satire and pastorals. Ibid.

3. The work "Gattung," the modern-day word for the French "genre," was still used in a general sense, such as when Scheibe, *Critischer Musikus* (1737; Leipzig, 1745), 40, writes about the "artificial or worked-out types [*Gattungen*] of counterpoints, fugues, canons and the like" or the "types of styles [*Gattungen der Schreibarten*], figures, arrangements and divisions." Scheibe restricted the word "Geschlecht" or gender to the three types of musical intervals.

4. For a detailed discussion of the historical baggage weighing down Johann Mattheson's uses of the word "style," see Claude Palisca, "The genesis of Mattheson's style classification," *New Mattheson Studies*, ed. George J. Buelow and Hans Joachim Marx (Cambridge: Cambridge University Press, 1983), 409-423.

5. Mattheson, *Der vollkommene Kapellmeister* (Hamburg, 1739) 72, English translation by Ernest Harriss, *Johann Mattheson's "Der vollkommene Kapellmeister"* (Ann Arbor: UMI Research Press, 1981). 196.

6. Scheibe, 669.

7. Scheibe details the "high style" on pp. 126-127. His stylistic hierarchy of high, middle, and low displays his intellectual allegiance to Johann Gottsched, particularly his *Versuch einer critischen Dichtkunst für die Deutschen* (Leipzig, 1730). See Palisca, 412.

8. Scheibe, 670.

9. Scheibe describes the middle style on pp. 128-129.

10. Another example concerns movements for the mass such as Kyries or Credos. Scheibe states (p. 169) that fugues are particularly appropriate, especially those making use of invertible counterpoint, canons and double fugues. First comes the genre—fugue—and then the appropriate manner of expressing it—the high style.

11. For a somewhat similar point of view, see Günter Wagner, "J.A. Scheibe — J.S. Bach: Versuch einer Bewertung," *Bach-Jahrbuch* 1982, pp. 33-49. Wagner, however, restricts Scheibe's criticism to Bach's sacred cantatas. But since Scheibe's notion of style is so broad, Wagner has probably interpreted the evidence too narrowly.

12. Scheibe, 134.

13. Scheibe, 646.

14. Scheibe, 148.

15. Preface, Peters edition (Leipzig, 1974), iii-iv.

16. Scheibe, 169.

17. Note what a genre is not: It is not a class of distinctive features with clear lines of demarcation from neighboring genres. Genre is historically, and hence, theoretically, looser than that. See Alastair Fowler, *Kinds of Literature: An Introduction to the Theory of Genres and Modes* (Cambridge, MA: Harvard University Press, 1982), much of whose discussion proceeds from this particular insight.

18. Spitta, *Johann Sebastian Bach*, 2 vols. (Leipzig, 1873, 1880), 2: 646.

19. Philipp Spitta, 2: 646. He excludes only "the impassioned Sarabande" from this criticism.

20. Wilhelm Fischer, "Zur Entwicklung des Wiener klassischen Stils," *Studien zur Musikwissenschaft* 3 (1915), 24-84.

21. Another straightforward example is the third movement of the first Brandenburg concerto.

22. See Roger Bullivant, "Fugue," *New Grove Dictionary of Music and Musicians*, 7: 15.

23. See, for example, ibid, 7: 12. "[W]hen the opening of a theme has been heard it is relatively unimportant if the whole of it is not reproduced, since attention is diverted by the other parts."

24. Lerner, 814.

Bach the Cantor, the Capellmeister, and the Musical Scholar: Aspects of the B-Minor Mass

Christoph Wolff

Nearly 170 years ago, in 1817, the Swiss critic and pub-lisher Hans-Georg Nägeli acclaimed Bach's B-minor Mass as the "greatest musical work of art of all times and of all peoples"[1]—an astonishing assertion at a time when the works of Mozart had already become a permanent feature of the musical landscape, and when Beethoven's fame was at its zenith. Conceptions of Johann Sebastion Bach in the early nineteenth cen-tury were hazy by comparison, the most common being that of a supreme master of fugue. He was best known as the composer of *The Well-Tempered Clavier* and of a substantial body of work for organ as well as of numerous four-part chorales and several motets, while the Bach of the great works for combined vocal and instrumental forces—particularly of the large-scale Passions and the Mass in B minor—remained almost totally unknown.

There was, it is true, a faint awareness of the existence of that unknown quantity; it can hardly have been entirely at random that Haydn, in his old age, took the trouble to acquire a manuscript copy of the B-minor Mass, or that around 1782/83 Mozart studied the work in preparation for his ambitious Mass in C minor, K. 427, which remained incomplete. Even the audience in Hamburg who heard C. P. E. Bach direct a performance of the Credo section from his father's Mass in 1784 was ready to acknowledge that it "had never heard before, and would probably never hear again" music of the like. Nevertheless, Nägeli's claim was essentially an intuitive judg-ment, but it had one not insignificant result, in that it challenged Beethoven, beginning in 1817/18 with the composition of the *Missa solemnis,* to emulate the dimensions of Bach's work in his own.

Time has taught us to be more cautious in the use of superlatives. A present-day critic would certainly not repeat Nägeli's pronouncement without qualification, though he would have to admit that it is not altogether preposterous. It is worth finding out, therefore, what it is about the work that makes it unique. In the last analysis, of course, only performance reveals the particular, unique nature of any musical work, but it can be useful to take historical factors into consideration as well, and establish certain factual correlations. The B-minor Mass, more than any other work, provides an example where the questions posed by a work are simultaneously a reflection of the many levels of complexity in the creator's artistic intentions. At the same time, unlike any other work of Bach's, the B-minor Mass permits us to gain insight into the wider context of this piece as the unquestionable culmination point of Bach's output of, and commitment to, sacred music. The Mass can only be understood on the background of his manifold activities as church musician, yet it reminds us even more specifically of the enormously broad base from which Bach operated as a musician in general.

The story of how the Mass came to be written would be quickly told if it amounted to nothing more than setting down the circumstances of the composition of its first section, the *Missa* (Kyrie and Gloria).[2] The Elector of Saxony and King of Poland, Augustus the Strong, died early in 1733, and a three-month period of mourning was ordered in Saxony, during which all musical performance was forbidden. This gave Bach a welcome period of leisure, which he seized upon as an opportunity for creative work: doubly welcome because he had in mind the highly practical purpose of commending himself to the new King-Elector with a work in his honor, in the hope of upgrading his position in Leipzig. His strategy was to write a piece of liturgical music acceptable to and important for the church music at the Catholic court in Dresden—which meant that a Lutheran Passion Oratorio, for example, was out of the question. Bach's plan to procure, with the dedication of the *Missa* in July, 1733, a court title for himself did not meet with immediate success; it was not until 1736 that he reached his declared goal of an appointment as court composer, and the "Cantor zu St. Thomas und Director Musices Lipsiensis" was then officially promoted to titular "Court Capellmeister" to the Elector of Saxony and King of Poland.

"Careerism" often played an important, and perfectly legitimate, part in Bach's plans. His goal, however, consisted exclusively in gaining the freedom and flexibility he needed in order to achieve what he set out to do. He left the various positions in Arnstadt,

Möhlhausen, Weimar, and Cöthen primarily for reasons of all too limited musical possibilities.[3] In fact, around 1730 there was even the temptation—for reasons of a well-documented frustration with the town authorities[4]—to leave Leipzig. But whether or not the *Missa* of 1733 is to be understood as a camouflaged indication of Bach's readiness to accept a post at the Dresden court, or simply as a statement of intent to provide the court with compositions for "the church and for the orchestra," it is not a sufficient explanation of the phenomenon of the B-minor Mass.

For one thing, Bach was already a capellmeister twice over: he had kept the title conferred on him at Cöthen, and in 1729 the Duke of Weissenfels had duplicated it. Bach had been able to sign himself "Cantor and Capellmeister," whenever he so chose, since 1723. The two aspects of his profession were in fact closely connected, especially during the entire period of 27 years he spent in Leipzig. It had actually begun with his appointment as Cantor of St. Thomas's. When the city council in Leipzig met to appoint a successor to the diligent but unimpressive Johann Kuhnau, they found themselves confronting a fundamental question of principle: should they appoint a musician who was primarily a schoolmaster, or should they make a departure from the established practice? There was an ambitious majority on the council, whose primary concern when filling the more important municipal posts was with brightening the city's worthy but dull commercial image, and so the voting went in favor of the capellmeisters among the applicants, men of the stature of Telemann, Graupner, Fasch and Bach. Schoolmasters like Tufen, Steindorf and Rolle probably stood no real chance from the outset; today their names are but minor footnotes in the history of music. But let us skip the details of the tortuous process whereby the choice finally fell on Bach: he, the famous and widely recognized keyboard virtuoso, entered on his new post with the clear objective of performing the office of cantor as a capellmeister.[5]

The dual aspect of his appointment affected all his activities in it, beginning with the way he tackled the task of composing a whole new repertory of church cantatas. In contrast to the common practice of the time—some of Bach's contemporaries, such as Telemann and Stölzel, wrote ten, fifteen or even more annual cycles—he wrote only the comparatively small number of five cycles during the first few years of his term of office. This provided him relatively quickly with a working repertory, on which it was possible to rely in successive years. The great advantage, musically, was that he thereby avoided any effect of routine or of mass production. Bach composed

nearly 200 church cantatas, every one of which has a highly individual stamp. The chorale cantatas of his second cycle from 1724-25
represent a case in point and demonstrate his manifold intentions: to
create a homogeneous body of works in contrast to the usual "mixed
bag" of pieces; to base the repertoire on a textually as well as
musically unifying theme throughout the liturgical year (he rightly
found it in the principal church hymns); to present within this
unprecedented, most monumental undertaking a multiplicity of
compositional forms and *cantus firmus* treatments (overture, concerto, fugue, motet, etc.); and simply to explore the possibilities as
well as the limits of vocal and instrumental virtuosity.

Having the organizational skill to mobilize the best musicians in
the city, Bach built up the relatively small standard ensemble
attached to St. Thomas's and St. Nicholas's (eight salaried town
musicians with their "entourage" of apprentices and assistants) with
his own private students, friends, and family members. This enabled
him to perform works which made great demands in the way of
virtuosity, and to introduce ambitious innovations in the formal
layout of the cantata, going so far as to incorporate large-scale
concerto movements; the outstanding examples are the great sinfo-
nias with concertante organ with which some of the cantatas open.
But the origins even of such a work as the *St. Matthew Passion,*
though it is much larger in scale than any of the cantatas, can be
associated with Bach's unique endeavor to reshape the function and
the image of the office of cantor, and his own incorruptible and
uncompromising capellmeister mentality was not the least of the
motives behind that endeavor. It is perfectly feasible to regard the
St. Matthew Passion as belonging, up to a certain point, within the
scope of a cantor's office and activities, as a capellmeister would
practice them. The conception and execution of the work, however,
cannot be explained exclusively by reference to the cantor and
capellmeister poles of Bach's musical existence. Parallels for its
incomparable design exist only in the fundamentally different genre
of opera. The same is true of the Mass in B minor, to an even greater
degree.

Let us circumscribe the subject a little more narrowly by first
turning our attention to the *Missa* of 1733, that is, the Kyrie and
Gloria which eventually formed the first section of the later Mass in
B minor. One of the duties of the cantor at St. Thomas's was to
perform a figural Kyrie, Gloria, and Sanctus, as well as a cantata, on
major church feasts. During his first few years in Leipzig, Bach met
this obligation by performing Latin pieces composed by others. Only

with the *Missa* of 1733 did his capellmeister instinct stir him to write something which put new life into the long-established traditions of the genre. This is apparent not only in the unusual requirement for a five-part choir and the exceptionally rich orchestration, but also, and especially, in the immense length of the work: Kyrie and Gloria together last an hour!

The sovereign skill with which the experienced capellmeister employed all the means of musical virtuosity in order to infuse his form with variety in abundance while preserving the architectonic integrity of a large-scale work can be demonstrated particularly by reference to the Gloria. Its four great solo movements each throw a spotlight on the representatives of the four principal orchestral sections in turn: the solo violin in the "Laudamus te," the solo flute in the "Domine deus," the oboe d'amore in the "Qui sedes" and the horn in the "Quoniam tu solus sanctus"; in each case the solo instrument is given a highly individual accompaniment by the rest of the ensemble—this is especially prominent in the blend of the horn and two bassoons in the "Quoniam." Incidentally, the five vocal soloists are also evenly represented; the fact that there are only four arias to accommodate five singers made it necessary to design one aria as a duet. Thus, it can easily be shown how finished, how well-rounded the *Missa* of 1733 was, and that the decision to expand the work beyond its original scope had to take into consideration the high degree of architectonic sophistication already achieved.

The later stages in the history of the B-minor Mass[6] reveal further perspectives, for in the last decade of his life Bach took up the 1733 *Missa* again and, by the addition of a Credo, Sanctus and Osanna, Benedictus, Agnus Dei and Dona nobis pacem, completed a mass cycle in accordance with the historical precedents, but clearly going beyond the boundaries of the Lutheran tradition. This was accomplished by means of an extraordinary mixture of newly-composed material with existing music which Bach revised for its new role. What is even more remarkable is that he did it for no discernible practical purpose. It was completely out of the question that a complete mass of this nature, a so-called "Missa tota," could be performed in a Protestant church: the fundamental tenet of Lutheran doctrine, that the sinner is justified by faith alone, meant that many sections of the Roman rite had to be excised from the evangelical liturgy. Only the singing of the Sanctus and Agnus Dei had been retained, although in a modified liturgical context. On the other hand, Bach's Mass was also unusable in the Catholic rite, not only on account of its departures from the prescriptive Latin text, but also, and in particular, because of the liturgically impermissible layout of the closing sections. All this is quite apart from the work's gigantic dimensions, which burst all liturgical bounds, Catholic or Protestant.

If, therefore, there could be no thought of this monumental work being performed within the context of a church service, what reasons can Bach have had for writing it? The question acquires greater significance from the fact that during that same final decade of his life he neglected important projects which had a direct liturgical application in order to work on his Mass. He had begun to revise the *St. John Passion*, for example, only to put it aside again. (Strictly speaking, the *St. John Passion* was never really finished. In particular, the chorale movements after No. 10 are in a detectably older style.)[7] It is recognized that Bach made hardly any totally new additions to the sacred music repertory in the 1740s—though it is a mistake to look on that as a sign of apathy. Bach betrayed few signs of having grown tired of his job, but he spent his time on things which interested him, even if there was no immediate necessity to write them; he worked above all on the realization of ideas which, though far from foreign to his office, were not intimately related to it. It was no longer the case that his activity as a composer was caught in the field of polar tension between the cantor's duties and the capellmeister's aspirations.

The same can be said, *mutatis mutandis*, of the instrumental compositions of the later years. There is, for example, Part Three of the *Clavier-Übung*, sometimes misleadingly entitled "The Organ Mass," which has a strong inner affinity to the Mass in B minor. Published in 1739, it brings together a collection of organ chorales of the highest artistic quality, the German Kyrie and Gloria and the six Lutheran Catechism hymns; but they do not possess an immediate liturgical function. The Mass and Catechism chorales are also not bound by the church year but, instead, applicable any time. Here, in the format of a "great organ book," which patently surpasses his very functional "little organ book," the Orgelbüchlein of so many years earlier, Bach presented the *summa* of his art as an organist, undoubtedly in the awareness that much therein would be technically and musically beyond the reach of the average organist. This *summa* effectively represents, in obvious analogy to the Catechism hymns chosen for the collection, his own "catechism" of organ composition and organ playing and is dedicated expressly to "the spiritual delectation of the lovers and, especially, the connoisseurs of this kind of work."[8]

From there, it is only a short step to the possibility of viewing the Mass in B minor as the *summa* of Bach's vocal composition, intended to be appreciated in particular by the "connoisseurs of this kind of work." The genre of the mass was especially suitable for an undertaking of such a nature, but at the same time it led "Cantor and Capellmeister" Bach into new regions of conceptual thought.

More traditions attach to the mass than to any other form of vocal music, and it has indeed been regarded since the fourteenth century as the central genre of sacred vocal music, so it is not surprising if Bach wanted to write his own contribution to this particular chapter of the history of music. The attraction must have been intensified by his awareness that the area of vocal music where he had always been most active, the cantata, was affected by the passage of time. Anyone could see how fashions came and went, how one type of cantata was replaced by another. The mass, in complete contrast, stood above time and fashion.

Furthermore, the mass was the pre-eminent choral genre, rather than a vehicle for solo singers. This is one of the principal differences between it and, for instance, the Passion or the oratorio, in which the element of solo singing has always been dominant. By contrast, the mass lays emphasis on the choir and its contribution, and gives the composer the chance to range across the entire spectrum of choral writing. For example, consider the absence in the mass of recitative. In consequence, there is a sense in which the B-minor Mass can be regarded, at least in part, as a kind of "specimen book" of vocal music, for it provides exemplars of a diversity of forms and techniques far richer than is offered by Bach's Passions, for instance, with their predilection for monody.

A number of factors bear out this hypothesis of the B-minor Mass as a specimen book. First, there is the matter of the principle governing the selection of the material included in it: the high standard Bach applied is demonstrated above all in the way he took the best material from existing masses, or mass sections, in order to show it off as exemplary. That the mass he chose for "completion" after 1740 was the *Missa* in B, rather than one of the *Missae breves* (in A major, G major, G minor and F major, BWV 233-236) which he had composed in the interim, is significant: the oldest of these five works was also the largest in scale and the best. The Sanctus of the Mass in B minor, again, is the oldest of his settings of this text and also, and more importantly, the most generously proportioned and the most polished: it is his Sanctus in D, which dates back from Christmas 1724 and represents, hence, the earliest piece of the Mass.

Its numerous parody movements—i.e., those using music which was originally written for other texts—were also chosen for their intrinsic musical quality. No doubt it would often have been easier for Bach to write a completely new movement, and the fact that he did not in, for example, the cases of the "Crucifixus" and the Agnus Dei testifies to a belief that the existing music possessed a substance and a potential which had not yet been fully exploited. This is borne out by the transformation which the passacaglia "Weinen, Klagen, Sorgen, Zagen," from the cantata BWV 12 composed at Weimar, in 1714, undergoes in its new guise as "Crucifixus" of the Mass, where it is both more refined and more profound in its content. It is not just a matter of the greater refinement of the instrumentation but rather, and more potently, the subtle and above all expressive rhetoric, such as shapes the setting of the concluding words "et sepultus est," with a sudden *a cappella* texture[9] and a modulation from E minor to G major.

In the realm of contrapuntal technique, the spectrum ranges from the concerto form of the "Gloria in excelsis" to the motet form of the "Gratias," from the modern concertante fugue of the "Et in terra pax" to the archaicizing fugue of the second Kyrie, from the freely expressive "Et incarnatus" to the strict canonic design of the "Confiteor," to give only a handful of examples from the choral numbers. But the same diversity can be observed in the solo numbers, in which Bach rigorously eschews the usual and fashionable *da capo* principle. Moreover, the overall structure of the Symbolum Nicenum (the Credo section), for instance, does not represent musical variety as such but a well-organized, in fact a logically controlled and symmetrically arranged sequence of nine movements: 2 choruses juxtaposing old and new styles, 1 solo, 3 choruses (with "Crucifixus" as center piece), 1 solo, 2 choruses again juxtaposing old and new styles.[10]

It would, of course, be a serious misconception to interpret the work as some kind of theoretical "treatise." Bach's thinking was entirely practical, even if the possibility of a complete performance of the Mass in his lifetime was nonexistent. There is no other way of interpreting the consistently cyclic nature of the work's design than by acknowledging that Bach was intent on inner integrity and an architectural design on the large scale. The musical return of the "Gratias" in the "Dona nobis pacem" is one witness to this, but there are more subtle ones—for instance, the juxtaposition of the deliberately contrived low ending of the Agnus Dei (as compared with the opening ritornello) to the beginning of the "Dona nobis pacem," which climbs up out of the depths and, thereby, provides a strong, *attacca*-type link. The disposition of tonalities in the whole of this final section also confirms the idea of a cyclic plan: D major (Osanna); B minor (Benedictus); G minor (Agnus Dei); D major (Dona nobis pacem). Bach might well, in fact, have put his Agnus Dei, in the key of F# minor or B minor; but for the sake of harmonic variety he deliberately chose the subdominant G minor, the only flat-side key in the entire work. In doing so he not only added a dimension that the heavily D-major oriented work to this point clearly lacked, namely tonal variety, he also simultaneously created a tonal reference to the only extended "flat" area in the preceding movements: the modulating episode at the conclusion of the "Confiteor," at the entrance of the words "Et exspecto resurrectionem mortuorum."

There is another reason for Bach's turning to the mass, with all its weight of historical tradition. This is the consciousness of his own position in history, a particularly characteristic phenomenon. In 1735, that is, around the time of his fiftieth birthday, Bach wrote down a family genealogy in which he recorded his own place in the succession of the generations of the Bachs, the Thuringian family of musicians, which had already produced several noteworthy composers in the seventeenth century, while by the 1730s, as Bach could see, his sons were getting ready to continue the tradition. He himself had cherished the inheritance of his forebears—in particular, he regularly performed the motets of his uncles Johann Christoph and Johann Michael Bach—and he even formed an "archive" of Bach family manuscripts. There can be no doubt that he had a keen awareness of history, both past and future, at least in the microcosm of his own family.

So, as he grew older, the B-minor Mass must have seemed to him to be a bequest to his successors and to the future. The concern to complete and perfect it preoccupied him virtually until the end of his life.[11] He had long ceased to attach importance to carrying out the *Thomascantor's* workload of adding new compositions to the repertory of "routine" church music, and no longer had much interest in the fulfillment of personal ambitions as a capellmeister as indicated by his withdrawal, after 1740, from the activities of the Collegium musicum. His primary interest now lay in the pursuit of "musical science," and the fulfillment of the scholar-composer's obligation to formulate a *summa* of his art. *The Art of Fugue* was the outcome in the field of instrumental music, and the Mass in B minor

in that of vocal composition: in assembling these two great collections, Bach anchored his own achievement firmly in the bedrock of
musical tradition. His grasp of that tradition went back to Palestrina,
whose *Missa sine nomine* was certainly a factor (together with his
study of other composers' mass scores) in the inspiration for the B-
minor Mass itself, and beyond Palestrina to the Gregorian *cantus
firmus* on which the "Credo in unum Deum" and "Confiteor" are
based.[12]

The Mass in B minor appears to be the *summa* not only of Bach's
vocal music, but of all his sacred music. Thus the text, of all sacred
texts, is the one that could not date, that had the paramount claim to
universal validity, overriding all confessional and linguistic boundaries. Setting this text of the mass meant, above all else, giving a
direct musical expression, without ambivalence, to invocation,
praise, and the confession of faith. Such an undertaking could not
but be close to Bach's heart, for it was the supreme opportunity to
unite his creed as a Christian with his creed as a musician in a single
statement. But that statement had to meet his own very highest
standards of perfection, and so it is no wonder that it took him more
than 15 years, from 1733 to around 1748, to complete. There was,
after all, no deadline: in this task the only obligation Bach ack-
nowledged was his personal responsibility to his creator, to tradition
and to posterity.

While there is no difficulty in seeing how the cantatas, the passions
and the oratorios fall within the scope of a cantor's duties as conceived and executed by a capellmeister, the phenomenon of the
Mass in B minor cannot be explained without some reference to the
reflective and scholarly dimension of Bach's musicianship. A complex system of thought at many levels went into the making of this
great Mass, and lifts it not only above the rest of his *oeuvre* but also
above the entire repertory of Western music. Nägeli's acclamation,
discussed at the beginning of this essay, seems to have been inspired
by an awed sense of this universal claim which Bach's B-minor Mass
makes unchallenged to this day.

Notes

1) A facsimile of the leaflet announcing Nägeli's project of the first publication of Bach's B-minor Mass is provided in F. Smend, "Kritischer Bericht," *Neue Bach-Ausgabe,* vol. II/1 (1954).

2) For a summary of the events that led to Bach's composition and dedication of the *Missa* see H.-J. Schulze, Preface to his facsimile edition of the original set of parts for the *Missa in h* (Leipzig, 1983).

3) Cf. C. Wolff, "Problems and New Perspectives of Bach Biography," *Proteus. A Journal of Ideas,* 2 (1985): 1-7.

4) *The Bach Reader* (H. T. David and A. Mendel, ed.), New York 1945, rev. ed. 1966, 120-124.

5) Cf. U. Siegele, "Bachs Stellung in der Leipziger Kulturpolitik seiner Zeit," *Bach-Jahrbuch,* 1983, 7-50; 1984, 7-43.

6) For a summary of the completion of the B-minor Mass after 1733 see A. Dürr, Afterword to his facsimile edition of Bach's autograph score (Kassel, 1966).

7) Cf. A. Mendel, "Kritischer Bericht," *Neue Bach-Ausgabe,* vol. II/3 (1970).

8) Cf. C. Wolff, "J. S. Bach's Clavier-Übung, Part III," *Gedenkschrift for Charles Brenton Fisk, Organbuilder* (in press).

9) A similar and closely related feature of dropping the instrumental accompaniment occurs in conjunction with Christ's last words ("Eli, Eli, lama Sabachthani") in the *St. Matthew Passion.*

10) The symmetry of this nine-movement arrangement was arrived at only as a result of a revision of the original eight-movement sequence after the completion of the Symbolum Nicenum: Bach assigned the text "Et incarnatus est," which first belonged to the Aria "Et in unum Deum," to a separate choral movement.

11) On the new datings of the *Art of Fugue* (originating in an early version around 1740) and the later parts of the B-minor Mass (representing Bach's last major compositional efforts) see C. Wolff, "Zur Chronologie und Kompositionsgeschichte von Bachs Kunst der Fuge," *Beiträge zur Musikwissenschaft,* 1983: 130-142, and Y. Kobayashi, "Zur Chronologie von Bachs Spätwerk," *Bericht über die wissenschaftliche Konferenz "Johannn Sebastian Bach. Weltbild, Menschenbild, Notenbild, Klangbild,"* Leipzig 1985 (in press).

On Bach's Universality

Robert L. Marshall

number of years ago I was asked to revise the article on "Bach, Johann Sebastian" for the fifteenth edition of the *Encyclopaedia Britannica*. One of the guidelines was to begin not with the conventional "J. S. Bach was born at Eisenach in Thuringia on March 21, 1685" and so on but with a "Statement of Significance." I decided to put it this way: "Although he was admired by his contemporaries primarily as an outstanding harpsichordist, organist, and expert on organ building, Johann Sebastian Bach is now generally regarded as one of the greatest composers of all time and is celebrated as the creator of the *Brandenburg Concertos*, *The Well-Tempered Clavier*, the *Mass in B minor*, and numerous other masterpieces of church and instrumental music. Appearing at a propitious moment in the history of music, Bach was able to survey and bring together the principal styles, forms and national traditions that had developed during preceding generations and, by virtue of his synthesis, enrich them all."[1]

There is nothing particularly original about this assessment, nor— I'm relieved to say— is it in any way incorrect. But I do believe now that it does not really do full justice to the magnitude of Bach's achievement. It subscribes, first of all, to the traditional view that Bach was "the culmination of an era"—to cite the subtitle of Karl Geiringer's well-known study of the composer[2]—or, in Albert Schweitzer's famous comment: "Bach is a . . . terminal point. Nothing comes from him; everything merely leads up to him."[3]

Now, about ten years ago, in an essay entitled "Bach the Progressive,"[4] I tried to demonstrate that Bach's "synthesis" was, if anything, even more extensive than was commonly appreciated—that his music constituted not only a "culmination" or a "terminal point" but often enough reflected the most advanced stylistic currents of his

time. Two of Bach's most monumental and serious works in particular—the Mass in B minor and the so-called "Goldberg" Variations—
both written relatively late in the composer's career, could be shown
to be indebted almost as much to the new, light, "pre-classic" or
"galant" style associated with the generation of Bach's sons—and
normally taken to be the very antithesis of Bach's personal style—as
they were to the venerable contrapuntal traditions of the preceding
century. I was arguing, in effect, that Bach's synthesis did not only
extend historically into the *past* and geographically to embrace the
great European national traditions of France, Italy, and Germany,
but that it also sought to encompass the most recent stylistic devel-
opments—to look *forward* as much as in any other artistic direction.
In other words, Bach's music seemed at times to aspire to, and to
achieve, a *universality* of style and idiom that was considerably
more far-reaching—and in fact more deliberate—than had hitherto
been recognized.

I wish at this time to pursue the notion of Bach's "universality"
more fully and to explore its specific implications for our understanding of his art.

I should emphasize that I am not primarily concerned here with
the question of the universality of Bach's *appeal*. But it might be
good to begin by asking whether the appeal of Bach's music is in fact
really all that general. With a few notable exceptions, his music is
certainly not as *popular* as that of, say, Beethoven or Mozart, not to
mention Tschaikovsky—although that situation might have changed
by the end of 1985. But if it did, I would expect it to be a temporary,
and most easily explanable, phenomenon. For the fact is that Bach's
music by and large is considerably less accessible to the typical
music lover than is that of the other major composers of history; nor
was it ever intended or expected to appeal to a concert audience in
the modern sense, that is, to a large, and, musically considered,
minimally educated, assembly of essentially passive listeners. It is
important to remember that commercial concert life for the general
public was only in its infancy by the end of Bach's life, and that Bach
accordingly had little occasion—although there was some—to write
what we may call "public" music.

It is possible, in fact, and rather profitable in many ways, to
consider Bach's music in terms of its function, or, what is to a great
extent the same thing, in terms of its intended audience. In fact, such
a functional classification of music was common at Bach's time—but
I hasten to add that contemporary commentators did not recognize
such a category as "public" music but rather divided musical activity

into three principal realms or institutions: the church, the chamber, and the theater. In the eyes of his own contemporaries, accordingly, Bach could hardly have been regarded as a "universal" composer by any means, since, strictly speaking, he wrote no music at all for the theater, that is, operas or ballets—although the argument certainly could be made that there is more genuine musical drama in many of his church compositions than in any opera of his time.

I should like to pursue the notion of "public" music a little further, though, and suggest that Bach's most generally appealing, i.e., his most popular music today, falls into one or the other of two categories, both belonging to that sphere: on the one hand, the free toccata or fantasia for the organ or some other keyboard instrument (which his contemporaries would quite properly have considered a species of church music); on the other hand, the instrumental concerto, regarded at the time as music for the chamber. Common to both forms, however, is an emphasis not only on virtuosity and, exuberant technical display—that is, on a readily appreciated sort of artistic prowess—and individualism—but also, often enough, on an intensity and, immediacy of expression that strikes a sympathetic listener as "personal" in tone and feeling. I am thinking of course of such works as the famous Toccata and Fugue in D minor for organ and the Brandenburg Concertos.

Needless to say, I do not in any way wish to disparage these genuinely grandiose works. They are not only supremely successful but in fact represent the epitome of compositions of their kind. And they are all quintessentially and unmistakably "Bachian" in the vigor and vitality of their rhythms, the boldness and originality of their harmonies, the richness and complexity of their colors and textures. And nowhere is Bach's music more searingly intense, more deeply "personal," if you will, than in the slow movement, say, of the First Brandenburg Concerto, or just about any other slow movement from a Bach concerto, for that matter.

There is surely no need to remind you how the Toccata in D minor goes; and I am confident that you can call to mind the brilliance and excitement, and also the poignant expressivity, of a Bach concerto. Virtually any movement from any Bach concerto, indeed, is music eminently well designed to excite and exhilarate or to move and grip the attentive and responsive listener who would have heard it in Bach's day, as he does today, as a member of an audience—no matter whether as an invited and privileged guest in the aristocratic salon or "chamber" of, say, the Margrave of Brandenburg or in the less exclusive surroundings of Herr Zimmermann's Coffee House in

Leipzig where the members of the local Collegium musicum would have performed such music under the direction of the composer. That is, the music would have been performed, then, as now, for an audience, and as part of a concert.

But barely two dozen concertos by Bach have survived, and—even if one adds the four orchestral suites (or overtures) which are in many ways similar and almost as popular—this would still obviously constitute a very small fraction of the close to eleven hundred compositions from his pen that have come down to us. As for the Toccata in D minor: its immense popularity is not only quite unique among Bach's organ works but, sorry to say, probably owes more to the extravagant arrangements of Leopold Stokowski and others and to Hollywood's exploitation of it in such movies as Walt Disney's *Fantasia* and *20,000 Leagues under the Sea* than it does to its own considerable, inherent interest. And much the same is true for Bach's other "great hits:" the so-called "Air for the G-String," the aria "Sheep may safely graze," or the chorale "Jesu, joy of man's desiring": they are typically lifted from their original contexts and often enough outfitted for an entirely different medium from the one prescribed by the composer.

Of Bach's close to 200 church cantatas, on the other hand, which represent the largest single body of compositions in his output, I doubt whether more than a handful have established themselves securely in today's musical life. But this is, really, quite understandable. For these works, for all their superb technical craftsmanship and profound expressivity, are not at all "public music" as I have just defined that term. Moreover, they were clearly designed to have anything other than a "universal" appeal. Indeed, they are, if you will, Bach's most "parochial" works, written for a completely circumscribed audience: not only, in the first instance, for an orthodox Lutheran congregation but specifically for one thoroughly familiar with the particular repertory of hymns, local liturgical traditions, and theological outlook prevailing in early eighteenth-century Leipzig. It is inevitable, I should think, that the modern listener has difficulty with this, quite frankly, rather alien repertoire: difficulty not only with the theological content, and especially, the rather drastic imagery of the texts, but also with some of the basic *musical* conventions of the genre—which (as it happens) were largely imported from the even more alien world of early eighteenth-century opera: the fairly regular succession and alternation of recitatives and arias, for example, and the apparently relentless repetition schemes associated with the all-pervasive da-capo principle of aria construction—a device which often renders the individual arias—for all their intrinsic beauty and effectiveness if heard separately—simply too long and, to our taste, too static in the context of a complete church cantata. In short, such compositions were not intended primarily for the "delectation" of a concert *public,* but rather for the "edification" of a church *congregation.* Indeed, from the composer's own point of view, they may have been conceived for and dedicated to the ultimately exclusive audience; for almost every one of Bach's cantata manuscripts closes with the inscription: *SDGl (Soli Deo Gloria),* i.e., to God alone the glory. Bach's cantatas, in fact, were conceived and should be regarded not as concert pieces at all but as musical sermons; and they were incorporated as such in the regular Sunday church services. I am reminded at this point of a remark by the Swiss theologian (and passionate Mozart enthusiast) Karl Barth which goes as follows: "It may or may not be the case that when the angels make music in praise of God they play Bach; but I am sure that when they are by themselves they play Mozart—and then God, too, is especially eager to listen in."[5]

In contrast to the regular Sunday cantatas, Bach's most monumental, and inspired, church compositions (the St. John and St. Matthew Passions, the Christmas Oratorio, the Mass in B minor) are not only recognized and appreciated as towering masterpieces but are performed regularly and frequently. In the case of the Passions and the Oratorio, I suspect it is not only the power of Bach's settings but also the inherent—and genuinely universal—drama of the biblical narratives at their core—in addition of course to their association with the major religious holidays, that have eased their way into our musical life. But even here I can't quite erase the suspicion that their frequent performance during the holidays may in fact be as much an act of musical piety as a sign of popular audience appeal. With the B-minor Mass, however, I believe the explanation is not the same; for it is not only immediately accessible but positively thrilling with its brilliant and utterly majestic choruses, the grace and straightforward lyricism of its solos and duets, and its unusually colorful and varied orchestral palette. Above all, the Mass is entirely free of those problematic baroque conventions of text and form that I mentioned before. The Mass in B minor is indeed a *catholic* work in every sense of the word, and as such occupies a unique place in Bach's *oeuvre,* one that gives it special significance in any consideration of the composer's universality.

I imagine that it is unnecessary for me to say that I have no doubt at all that even the few works of Bach for which I have just conceded broad popular "audience" appeal—the concertos, Passions, the Christmas Oratorio and the B-minor Mass—provide ample testimony of his genius and would guarantee a prominent place for him in the pantheon even if no other compositions of his had survived. But it seems to me that the actual source of Bach's supreme stature at the pinnacle of Western culture lies elsewhere. It is to be found in those works that, quite obviously, I'm sure, I have deliberately avoided mentioning up to now—the awesome collections of instrumental music: the compositions for unaccompanied violin or cello, the various chamber sonatas for flute, or violin, or viola da gamba and harpsichord; and, of course, the keyboard masterpieces: the French and English suites, the partitas, the Goldberg Variations, the miniature gems of the *Orgelbüchlein* as well as the grander chorale preludes and fantasies, and above all the sublime preludes and fugues that reach a veritable apotheosis in the two volumes of the *Well-Tempered Clavier,* the *Musical Offering,* and his final musical testament: *Die Kunst der Fuge (The Art of Fugue).*

I did not mention these works before because, with the possible exception of the Goldberg Variations, they are *not* "public" works aimed at a *listening* "audience." Unlike the fundamentally *dramatic* conception that underlies the concerto (and, to some extent, the toccata and fantasia) which is based on a *dualistic* principle emphasizing and exploiting contrasts and juxtapositions of all kinds—first of all, the inherently dramatic opposition of solo and tutti which brings in its wake sharp contrasts of dynamics, rhythms, melodic ideas, instrumental textures, harmonies, and even keys—most of Bach's instrumental music is governed by an aesthetic principle that was known at the time as the "unity of affect," according to which a composition was to be governed and unified by a single emotion or mood. This premise led, in Bach's case, to a veritably breathtaking logic and consistency in the development of musical ideas that has never been surpassed or perhaps even equaled since. The dualistic principle of composition was to reach its culmination in the classical era: in the sonata forms of Haydn, Mozart, and Beethoven. The *dramatically* conceived masterpieces of these composers—the string quartets of Haydn, the operas of Mozart, the sonatas and symphonies of Beethoven—epitomize, if you will, music as an art of personal *communication;* the *logically* conceived preludes and fugues of Bach, it seems to me, are, by contrast, in the first instance an art of *revelation.* Accordingly, they belong, primarily, not in a recital hall—or even in an eighteenth-century salon or "chamber"— but on one's own music stand. They are not so much meant to be merely "listened" to, but to be played—and studied. In this, Bach's position in our musical life is absolutely unique. His most profound appeal is not to the "general" or even "sophisticated" *public* but to the *initiated*—by which I mean, quite frankly, to fellow musicians. This does not mean that one literally has to earn one's living as a professional musician in order to appreciate, and love, Bach's music. But I would venture the guess that almost all of Bach's most devoted admirers today, as in the past, developed their admiration—indeed their almost physical need—for his music not by hearing it per-formed (on records or at concerts—no matter) but by playing it, or perhaps singing it, themselves and thereby entering actively into an aesthetic realm of a particularly sublime, transcendental, sort. This is a quite different experience from that of allowing oneself to be emotionally moved, be it ever so deeply, by more—shall we call them—worldly, or "human" sentiments transmitted, that is "com-municated," by intermediaries: by professional "interpreters."

The sense of actively participating in something transcendental, when we play or intensively listen to Bach's music, I maintain, is central to understanding his position in our culture. Pablo Casals once said:

> For the past eighty years I have started each day in the same manner. It is not a mechanical routine but something essential to my daily life. I go to the piano, and I play two preludes and fugues of Bach. I cannot think of doing otherwise. It is a sort of benediction on the house. But that is not its only meaning for me. It is a rediscovery of the world of which I have the joy of being a part. It fills me with awareness of the wonder of life, with a feeling of the incredible marvel of being a human being. The music is never the same for me, never. Each day it is something new, fantastic and unbelievable. That is Bach, like nature, a miracle.[6]

But I think Goethe came even closer to the essence when he wrote in a letter to a friend after having heard the preludes and fugues of the *Well-Tempered Clavier* for the first time: "I expressed it to myself as if the eternal harmony were communing with itself, as might have happened in God's bosom shortly before the creation of the world."[7]

Perhaps it would be fair to say—in any case, it is the main point of this talk—that the notion of the universality of Bach's music acquires its profoundest meaning when it is understood, once again, not in terms of the universality of its appeal, its popularity, since, as I think I have made clear, such a claim could be credibly challenged, but when it is understood with reference to a kind of universal validity. And there is some evidence that Bach in fact conceived of his art, and also his artistic mission, in much this way. Of course, he would have put it far more modestly himself, and in fact did so, for example, on the title page of the *Well-Tempered Clavier* which he declared was "for the Use and Profit of the Musical Youth Desirous of Learning as well as for the Pastime of those Already Skilled in this Study." In a similar, if more playful, mode, he ended the title of his *Orgelbüchlein* with an ingenuous couplet that has been translated as "In Praise of the Almighty's Will / And for my Neighbor's Greater Skill."[8]

That is, it is quite clear that while Bach may not have thought of himself as a musical prophet, he certainly did very much think of himself as a teacher; and not only the title pages and prefaces of the *Well-Tempered Clavier,* and the *Orgelbüchlein* but those of the Two- and Three-part Inventions, and *Musical Offering,* and the *Art of Fugue* as well, all provide explicit testimony as to the didactic function of these monumental works. It would certainly not be difficult to argue, in fact, that Bach was the most self-consciously pedagogical of the great composers. An important implication of this is that Bach evidently regarded the pieces contained in these collections in the first instance as "exemplary" in the most literal sense: as *models*—to be studied and emulated—rather than, say, as divinely inspired and profoundly individual poetic or visionary statements that were intended to move his fellow man and perhaps even contribute to his spiritual or moral salvation. Unlike Beethoven, Bach did not claim to be a Bacchus who, for the sake of mankind, pressed immortal wine out of the grapes of art—even if he in fact did so.

Now just what did Bach think he was imparting in those didactic compositions? The title page of the Two- and Three-part Inventions reads as follows:

> Upright Instruction / wherein the lovers of the clavier, and especially those desirous of learning, are shown a clear way not alone (1) to learn to play clearly in two voices, but also, after further progress, (2) to deal correctly and well with three obbligato parts; furthermore, at the same time not alone to have good inventions [i.e, ideals] but to develop the same well, and above all to arrive at a singing style in playing and at the same time to acquire a strong foretaste of composition.[9]

Evidently Bach was convinced that virtually everything in the "craft" of music was teachable and learnable. He is supposed to have remarked on one occasion: "I have had to work hard; anyone who works just as hard will get just as far."[10] For music, even first-class music, was not so much the product of divine inspiration granted to the rare genius, but was rather the product of the proper application of certain fundamental principles—principles that Bach seems to have regarded as eternal, that is, as God-given, verities. He once expressed his sentiments on the thorough bass, for example, as follows:

> The thorough bass is the most perfect foundation of music, being played with both hands in such manner that the left hand plays the notes written down while the right adds consonances and dissonances, in order to make a well-sounding harmony to the Glory of God and the permissible delectation of the spirit; and the aim and final reason, as of all music, so of the thorough bass should be none else but the Glory of God and the recreation of the mind. Where this is not observed there will be no real music but only a devilish hubbub.[11]

It seems to me that such phrases as "the most perfect foundation of music," "a well-sounding harmony to the Glory of God," "the aim and final reason of all music," "otherwise no real music but a devilish hubbub" all document Bach's conviction that music—real music, at all events—is constructed according to God-given, that is, eternally and *universally* valid, principles, call them "laws"; and with his systematically organized collections of keyboard music and their explicitly didactic prefaces, Bach's main, but certainly not sole, purpose, apparently, was to demonstrate these universal musical laws in operation. The *Well-Tempered Clavier,* for example, explores both the potentials of a newly established tuning procedure which, for the first time in the history of keyboard music, made all the keys equally usable, and, more significantly, the possibilities for musical organization afforded by the system of "functional tonality," a kind of musical syntax consolidated in the music of the Italian concerto composers of the preceding generation and a system that was to prevail for the next 200 years. The basic principle of this "tonal" system has been described as the creation of a sense of key-feeling by means of "sequences of chords that gravitated toward the tonal center. The degree of attraction depended on the distance of the chords from the tonic—i.e., the home key—and this distance was measured and determined by the circle of fifths [i.e., a series of dominant-tonic progressions that could encompass all the degrees of a particular scale or key.]"[12]

It would obviously lead us much too far afield to embark on a technical discussion of musical tonality. But I would like to point out that it evolved at just about the same time—in the 1680s, mainly in Italy in the music of Corelli and his contemporaries—that Isaac

Newton was giving final form to his theories of gravitation based on precise, and universal, laws and measurements of distance and motion. Both Newton's laws of the universe and the principles of musical tonality were obviously the product of the same Age of Reason into which Bach, like Newton, was born.

When I mentioned in the encyclopedia article which I quoted at the outset of this talk that Bach appeared at a propitious moment in the history of music, what I had in mind was his advent at the completely unique moment when the age-old traditions of counterpoint and polyphony intersected with the newly-established system of tonal harmony. Bach, more than any other composer of his time, or since, not only thoroughly perfected and advanced the techniques of both but fully realized the implications and the potential of their fusion. If I may pursue my analogy with natural science a bit further, I think it may be fair to say, that Bach's unification of linear counterpoint and tonal harmony represents an accomplishment in the art of music hardly less impressive than that which would be achieved if a physicist someday would realize Albert Einstein's hope of formulating a theory—a unified field theory—in which the nature of the relationships obtaining among the various forces at work in the cosmos—gravitation, magnetism, electricity, and so on—were precisely defined and established once and for all. But I suspect that I may be rushing in where angels properly fear to tread.

At all events, from the perspective of musical history synthesis and fusion are the hallmarks of Bach's achievement. Not only did he unify and reconcile the structural principles of harmony and polyphony but, as I remarked at the beginning, he also effected a synthesis of the most important national schools and traditions of Europe; and in this respect as well Bach's music betrays a "universal" ambition in its range and scope.

I have already mentioned that musical commentators of the early eighteenth century, like all writers of the Enlightenment age, were typically fond of categories, and I referred specifically to their division of music into the stylistic realms associated with the church, the chamber, and the theater. They had also developed a system of classification based on national distinctions, paticularly those that were to be observed between the dominant French and Italian styles: French instrumental music, for example, was characterized, among other things, by the dance and the dance suite and by profuse and delicate ornamentation; the instrumental music of Italy by the expansive formal designs of the sonata and the concerto and by the propensity for elaborate and extravagant improvisation. Critics were equally sensitive to the differences between Italian and French opera and their vocal styles: between the unabashedly sensuous melody and pyrotechnical display of the Italian aria, on the one hand, and the infinitely more serious, restrained, declamatory airs to be heard in the French *tragédie lyrique,* on the other. And we often find among the composers of the time rather self-conscious efforts to juxtapose and contrast these styles in their music. François Couperin, for example, published a collection of instrumental pieces which he called *Réunion des goûts*—a title awkward to translate but readily understood as the union, or unification of national tastes—and which included, among other things, minuets written in the contrasting styles of the Frenchman Jean-Baptiste Lully and the Italian Arcangelo Corelli.

As for Germany, it not only was exposed to and absorbed the stylistic and cultural influences emanating from France and Italy, and elsewhere, but was deeply conscious of that fact and concerned about how it affected its own cultural "identity," if you will. Bach once remarked: "It is . . . somewhat strange that German musicians are expected to be capable of performing at once and *ex tempore* all kinds of music, whether it came from Italy or France, England or Poland. . . ."[13]

Now Bach's mastery of the various national styles went far beyond mere cosmopolitan versatility: the ability to write French suites, Italian concertos, German fugues, or Polish polonaises. Such skills—and we can add to them his familiarity with and command of an impressive array of historical styles encompassing the medieval *cantus firmus* setting, the vocal motet of the Renaissance (referred to in Bach's day as the *stile antico*), and so on, on to the simple, but modish *galant* manner of the younger generation—all of this "encyclopedic competence" represented for Bach little more than a point of departure. For Bach's unique accomplishment was not that he had cultivated and totally mastered each of these forms and conventions but that he succeeded in galvanizing them into a single, coherent whole. That is, in an age that had conceived of music in terms of individual national traditions, and discrete stylistic, functional categories, Bach had managed to create a genuine synthesis: to forge a genuinely *universal* style. The "universality" of the *Well-Tempered Clavier,* for example, consists not only in its fusion of tonal and harmonic forces but also in that it constitutes a virtual compendium of the most important forms and styles of the era: dance types of all nations, Italianate arias, archaic motets, modernistic concertos, etc.,—*all developed in accordance with a single compositional principle: that of the venerable, and rigorous, fugue.*

Or consider the finale of the Fifth Brandenburg Concerto. It is, of course, a concerto movement, or more strictly speaking, a concerto grosso movement, since it employs a group of soloists—a flute, a violin, and a harpsichord—in alternation and combination with an accompanying "tutti" ensemble. But the movement is not only a manifestation of the (Italian) concerto principle. It is, at literally the same time, a (German) fugue—in its texture; a (French) dance (a gigue)—in its rhythm, meter and tempo; and a da capo aria (and thus indebted to the vocal as well as to the instrumental realm)—in its form.

Example 1: Brandenburg Concerto No. 5, BWV 1050:
    Opening of MOvement 3

But I can think of no more spectacular demonstration of Bach's powers of synthesis, his unparalleled combinatorial genius—all in the service, I submit, of a "universal" vision unprecedented in the history of Western music—than in one of his church compositions: specifically, in the opening chorus of the cantata *Jesu, der du meine Seele*, Cantata No. 78. Cantata 78 is "just another" Sunday cantata, part of a series that Bach had composed at the rate of about one per week over a period of approximately three years that had begun with his arrival in Leipzig in May of 1723. Cantata 78 was written in 1724 for the Fourteenth Sunday after Trinity, a day that fell on September 10. Since Bach had composed a new cantata the previous week (Cantata No. 33, first performed on the 13th Sunday after Trinity, September 3, 1724), he most likely wrote Cantata 78 in the week beginning on Monday, September 4. I imagine that Bach spent at most three or four days engaged in the composition of the entire work, for he would have had to leave a couple of days for the writing out of parts and for at least one rehearsal, I should think, before the performance on September 10. In short, I doubt whether Bach could have devoted more than one day—it must have been Monday, September 4—to the composition of the chorus I am about to discuss.

The movement is normally described as a chorale-fantasy chorus because it is an elaborate setting, for chorus, of a German "chorale," that is, a congregational hymn—in this instance the chorale *Jesu, der du meine Seele* (Jesus, Thou my weary spirit), by the seventeenth-century poet, Johann Rist. Bach's approach to the movement is a conventional one in that he presents the traditional melody of the chorale—in the soprano part—as a *cantus firmus*, that is, set distinctly apart from the surrounding voices and instruments. In adopting the melody of the chorale Bach also adopts its form: the so-called *Barform* consisting of a pair of lines or phrases that are repeated and then followed by new material. The form can be represented schematically as AAB. The melody of the Chorale goes as follows (as notated by Bach in the final movement of BWV 78):

Example 2: Chorale Melody: *Jesu, der du meine Seele*

Both the *Barform* and the *cantus-firmus* technique can be traced back to the Middle Ages: the *Barform* is found in the courtly love songs of the German *Minnesänger* as early as the twelfth century; the *cantus-firmus* technique formed the basis of the earliest examples of Western polyphony dating from the eleventh century or even earlier.

The lower voices of the chorus, for their part, offer a polyphonic commentary, in imitative texture, as in a fugue, on each line of the text preceding its entrance, along with the official hymn melody, in the soprano *cantus firmus*. This is a compositional principle associated with the renaissance motet of the sixteenth century, specifically, with that of the so-called *cantus-firmus* motet. (The imitation preceding the first line of the chorale goes as follows:)

Example 3: Cantata 78, Movement 1, mm. 15-23

Now these vocal episodes each consisting of the *cantus-firmus* melody in the soprano and its polyphonic preview in the lower voices are separated from one another by a refrain of sorts in the orchestra. This refrain, or ritornello, also appears at the beginning and end of the movement and thus provides a frame for the choral sections. The ritornello principle, in which a relatively constant theme or melody recurs in alternation with a succession of contrasting and changing episodes (such as the chorale phrases here), is the

controlling formal idea of the mature baroque concerto of the early
eighteenth century, as it was developed by Bach's slightly older
Italian contemporaries, in particular Giuseppe Torelli and Antonio
Vivaldi. The ritornello melody of our chorus, as it is presented at the
outset of the movement, goes as follows:

Example 4: Cantata 78, Movement 1, mm. 1-7

A most striking feature of this melody is its rhythm:

Example 5: Cantata 78, Movement 1, mm. 1-4: Rhythm

and also its regular phrase structure. Every phrase is exactly the
same length; they are all four measures long. In short, the ritornello
melody has the phrase structure of a dance and the rhythmic character, specifically, of the sarabande—one of the standard items in the
contemporary French dance suite.

There is one further, crucial, structural element in this movement,
one that pervades it virtually without interruption from beginning to
end: the ever-recurrent phrase first presented in the bass but later
appearing in other parts as well:

Example 6: Cantata 78, Movement 1, mm. 1-4: Continuo line

This is a *basso ostinato*—a relatively short phrase whose relentless repetitions provide the basis for the passacaglia or chaconne;
essentially a set of variations on a dance pattern whose origins can

be traced back to early seventeenth-century Spain. The particular *basso ostinato* Bach uses here with its rather mournful half-step descent from the tonic to the dominant is the so-called *lamento* bass frequently encountered in dirges and elegies in seventeenth-century opera. (The most well-known example today, no doubt—although it is inconceivable that Bach would have known it—is the lament, "When I am laid in earth" from Henry Purcell's opera *Dido and Aeneas*.)

In sum, *Jesu, der du meine Seele* is one of Bach's most complex creations—a compositional *tour de force* that simultaneously observes or fulfills no fewer than five distinct principles of organization, some of which, one would have thought, were mutually exclusive—such as the combination of the repetitive *basso ostinato* with the ongoing *cantus-firmus* melody. At one and the same time the movement is a modern, Italian, concerto—but based on a ritornello in the style of a sarabande from a modern French dance suite; it is a seventeenth-century passacaglia, i.e., a set of variations; but it is also a polyphonic motet constructed both on "points of imitation" reminiscent of renaissance church music of the sixteenth century as well as on a *cantus firmus* according to compositional principles extending back to the Middle Ages; on yet another level the movement is a German Lutheran chorale in *Barform*: AAB—writ very large indeed.

It is virtually impossible to imagine a grander, more comprehensive, more "universal" synthesis of historical and national styles than Bach has achieved in this movement—incorporating as it does elements of the secular as well as the sacred, the instrumental as well as the vocal; a movement whose frame of reference embraces both the Roman Catholic motet of the sixteenth century and the Lutheran chorale and whose procedures are indebted to the medieval *cantus-firmus* setting, the variation technique of the seventeenth-century passacaglia, and on to the modern Italian concerto and the French dance suite.

But Bach's achievement here is not only prodigious; it is in fact prophetic in its objective of transcending the cultural limitations of geography and history, of place and time, in order to create—once again— a "universal" artwork. For the outlook of his contemporaries, you will recall, was confined by their predilection to conceive of and divide musical practices and traditions along national and other lines. The idea of a universal musical style—of music as a universal language—was not to emerge for another half-century: during the

Classical period, in the 1770s and 1780s. The composer Christoph Willibald Gluck spoke in 1773 of his wish to write a music that "would appeal to all peoples" and "wipe out the ridiculous differences in national music." And he would have been gratified to read, a dozen years later, that his music represented "the universal language of our continent." Joseph Haydn once remarked, "My language is understood in the whole world."[14] The ultimate form of this universal musical language, admittedly, was not that pursued by Bach. It was rooted rather in the formal conventions and procedures of the basically Italian sonata colored by folk music idioms imported from many national and ethnic traditions and enriched with sophisticated harmonic and contrapuntal techniques inherited from the Germans—above all from Bach. The new, more popularistic, more democratic aesthetic ideal demanded a lightness, simplicity, and immediacy of appeal far removed from Bach's clearly contrapuntally inspired notion of a musical universality that was universal by virtue of being all-inclusive and all-encompassing: not so much a universal musical language as a musical "universe"—as Goethe had said: "as if the eternal harmony were communing with itself as might have happened in God's bosom shortly before the creation of the world."

Notes

1. Walter Emery and Robert L. Marshall, "Bach, Johann Sebastian," *Encyclopaedia Britannica*, 15th edition (Chicago, 1974), 2:556-61.

2. Karl Geiringer, *Johann Sebastian Bach: The Culmination of an Era* (New York, 1966).

3. Albert Schweitzer, *J. S. Bach*, translated by Ernest Newman (London, 1911), 3.

4. Robert L. Marshall, "Bach the Progressive: Observations on his Later Works," *The Musical Quarterly* 62 (1976): 313-57.

5. Karl Barth, *Wolfgang Amadeus Mozart* (Zurich, 1956), 12.

6. Pablo Casals and Albert E. Kahn, *Joys and Sorrows, Reflections by Pablo Casals as Told to Albert Kahn* (London, 1970), 17.

7. Postscript to a letter of 17 July 1827 addressed to Karl Friedrich Zelter.

8. Hans T. David and Arthur Mendel, *The Bach Reader*, revised ed. (New York, 1966), 85 and 75, respectively.

9. *The Bach Reader*, 86.

10. Ibid., 37.

11. Ibid., 32f.

12. Manfred F. Bukofzer, *Music in the Baroque Era* (New York, 1947), 220.

13. *The Bach Reader*, 123.

14. These quotations are cited in Friedrich Blume, *Classic and Romantic Music* (New York, 1970), 28.

Table I
Work Headings in the Primary Sources
of Bach's Organ Compositions*

BWV	Heading	Source	Date	Comment
525-30	Sonata 1[-6] à 2 Clav. et Pedal	P 271	c.1730	Autograph
535	Preludio con Fuga per il Organo	Lpz III. 8.7.	c.1740-50	Apograph w. autograph additions
535a	Praeludium cum Fuga - ex Gb. Pedaliter	Mus. ms. 40644	c.1707	Autograph fragment
541	Praeludium pro Organo con Pedal: obligat:	SPK (1983)	c.1733-42	Autograph
544	Praeludium pro Organo cum pedale obligato (Title page)	Private	c.1727-31	Autograph
	Praeludium in Organo pleno, pedal: (Heading)	Private	c.1727-31	Autograph
545	Praeludium pro Organo cum Pedale obligato (Title page)	lost	?	Autograph
	Praeludium in Organo pleno pedaliter (Heading)	lost	?	Autograph
548	Praeludium pedaliter pro Organo	P 274	c.1727-31	Partial Autograph (to m.21 of Fugue; thereafter: Kellner)
550	Praeludium pedaliter	P1210	?	Apograph w. autograph additions
552/1	Praeludium pro Organo pleno	Clavier Übung III	1739	Original Edition
552/2	Fuga à 5. con pedale. pro Organo pleno	Clavier Übung III	1739	Original Edition
562/1	Fantasia pro Organo. a. 5 Vocum, cum pedali obligato	P 490	c.1720-30	Autograph
562/2	Fuga. a 5	P 490	c.1745?	Autograph fragment

Table I (Continued)
Work Headings in the Primary Sources
of Bach's Organ Compositions*

BWV	Heading	Source	Date	Comment
573	Fantasia pro Organo	P 224	c.1722-23	Autograph
596	Concerto a 2 Clav: & Pedale	P 330	c.1713	Autograph
599-644	Orgel-Büchlein Worinne einem anfahenden Organisten Anleitung gegeben wird . . . sich im *Pedal studio zu habilitiren*, indem . . . das Pedal gantz obligat *tractiret wird*.	P 283	1713ff	Autograph title added during Köthen period
645-50	Sechs Chorale von verschiedener Art auf einer Orgel mit 2 Clavieren und Pedal. . . .	Print	c.1748	Original Edition
651-65	[From the "Seventeen Great Chorales"]	P 271	1740-48?	Autograph
651	Fantasia . . . in organo pleno			
652	alio modo à 2 Clav. et Ped			
653	a 2 Clav. e Pedal			
654	[ditto]			
655	Trio a 2 Clav. e Pedal			
656	Versus. manualiter [3rd Verse:] Pedal			
657	a 2 Clav. et Ped.			
658	[over Staff:] Ped.			

Table I (Continued)
Work Headings in the Primary Sources
of Bach's Organ Compositions*

BWV	Heading	Source	Date	Comment
659	a 2 Clav. et Ped.			
660	a due Bassi è canto fermo			
661	in organo pleno. Canto fermo in Pedal			
662	a 2 Clav. et Ped.			
663	[ditto]			
664	Trio ... a 2 Clav. et Ped			
665	sub communione ... pedaliter			*pedaliter* possibly added later
669-89, etc	Dritter Theil der Clavier Übung bestehend in verschiedenen Vorspielen über die Catechismus- und andere Gesaenge, vor die Orgel	Clavier Übung III	1739	Original Edition
669	à 2 Clave. et Ped			
670	[ditto]			
671	à 5 Canto fermo in Bassi cum Organo Pleno			
672	alio modo manualiter			
675	Canto fermo in alto			

Table I (Continued)
Work Headings in the Primary Sources
of Bach's Organ Compositions*

BWV	Heading	Source	Date	Comment
676	à 2 Clav. et Pedal			
677	. . . manualiter			
678	à 2 Clav. et Ped.			
679	. . . manualiter			
680	In Organo pleno con Pedali			
681	. . . manualiter			
682	à 2 Clave. et Pedal			
683	alio modo manualiter			
684	à 2 Clav. e Canto fermo in Pedal			
685	alio modo manualiter			
686	à 6 in Organo pleno con Pedale doppio			
687	à 4 alio modo manualiter			
688	à 2 Clav. e Canto fermo in Pedal			
689	à 4 manualiter			

Table I (Continued)
Work Headings in the Primary Sources
of Bach's Organ Compositions*

BWV	Heading	Source	Date	Comment
691	Wer nur den lieben Gott läßt walten	Yale: (Clavier-Büchlein WFB)	c.1720	Autograph
728	Jesus mein Zuversicht	P 224	c.1722-23	Autograph
739	Wie schön leuchtet . . . a 2 Clav. Ped.	P 488	c.1705?	Autograph
753	Jesu meine Freude	Yale: (Clavier-Büchlein)	c.1720	Autograph
764	[No Heading]	P 488	c.1705?	Autograph
769	Einige canonische Veraenderungen . . . vor die Orgel mit 2. Clavieren │ und dem Pedal	Print	c.1747?	Original Edition
769a	Von Himmel hoch . . . [Var. 1, 2, 4:] a 2 Clav. et Pedal	P 271	c.1748?	Autograph

* See the source descriptions in the pertinent Kritische Berichte of the NBA and Bach-Dokumente I; also Stauffer, The Organ Preludes, Appendix I, and Williams, The Organ Music, passim.

Table II
Work Headings in the Primary Sources
of Bach's "Klavier" Compositions**

BWV	Heading	Source	Date	Comment
772-801	[No General Title]	Yale Clavier-Büchlein	c.1722-23	Autograph
772-86	Preambulum 1 [-15] (Headings)			
787-801	Fantasia 1 [-15] (Headings)			Autograph
772-801	Auffrichtige Anleitung, Wormit denen Liebhabern des Claviores ... eine deütliche Art gezeiget wird .... eine cantable Art im Spielen zu erlangen	P 610	1723	Autograph
772-87	Inventio 1 [-15] (Headings)	P 610	1723	Autograph
788-801	Sinfonia 1 [-15] (Headings)	P 610	1723	Autograph
802-5	Duetto I [-IV]	Clavier Übung III	1739	Original Edition
814	Suite pour le Clavessin	P 224	1722	Autograph
815	Suite ex Dis pour le Clavessin	P 224	1722	Autograph
816	Suite pour le Clavessin ex G♭	P 224	1722	Autograph
825-30	Clavier Übung bestehend in Praeludien, Allemanden, Couranten, Sarabanden, Giquen, Menuetten, und andern Galanterien	Clavier Übung I	1731 (1726-30)	Original Edition
	[Individual Compositions] Partita I [-VI]			
827	[No Heading]	P 225	1725	Autograph

Table II (Continued)
Work Headings in the Primary Sources
of Bach's "Klavier" Compositions**

BWV	Heading	Source	Date	Comment
830	[No Heading]	P 225	1725	Autograph
831a	Ouverture pour le Clavesin	P 226	c.1730	Apograph w. autograph heading
971, 831	Zweyter Theil der Clavier Übung . . . vor ein Clavicymbel mit zweyen Manualen	Clavier Übung II	1735	Original Edition
846-69	Das Wohltemperirte Clavier, oder Praeludia, und Fugen durch alle Tone und Semitonia . . .	P 415	1722-c.40	Autograph
870-93	["Well-Tempered Clavier II": No Title page]	London BL Add. 35021	c.1738-41	Partially autograph
886	Fuga ex Gis dur	P 274	1730s	Autograph
906/1	Fantasia per il Cembalo	Bethlehem Bach Choir	1726-31	Autograph
906/1-2	[No Heading]	Dresden LB 2405-T-52	c.1735-40	Autograph fragment
924	Praeambulum 1	Yale Clavier-Büchlein	1720	Autograph
930	Praeambulum	Yale Clavier-Büchlein	1720-22	Autograph
953	Fuga à 3	Yale Clavier Büchlein	1724	Autograph
988	Clavier Übung bestehend in einer ARIA mit verschiedenen Veraenderungen vors Clavicimbal mit 2 Manualen. . . .	Clavier Übung [IV]	c.1742	Original Edition

Table II (Continued)
Work Headings in the Primary Sources
of Bach's "Klavier" Compositions**

BWV	Heading	Source	Date	Comment
991	Air	P 224	1722	Autograph
994	Applicatio	Yale Clavier-Büchlein	1720	Autograph

**See the source description in the pertinent Kritische Berichte of the NBA and Bach-Dokumente I, as well as the various published facsimile editions.

Table III

Representative Early Sources of Bach's Keyboard Toccatas

(by Key)

Key	BWV	Heading	Source	Comment
CM	564	Toccata ex C♮. pedaliter	P 286	Copyist: Kellner; range: to d″
Cm	911	Toccata C♭ Manualiter	ABB	Copyist: Hauptschreiber
DM	912a	Toccata ex D fis	Mus, ms. 40644	Copyist: Hauptschreiber
DM	912	Toccata. Manualiter del … Bach Organista	P 289	Anonymous copyist; 2nd half of 18th century
Dm	565	Toccata Con Fuga: pedaliter. ex d♯ [sic]	P 595	Copyist: Ringk
Dm	538	Toccata con Fuga Db	P 803	Copyist: Walther
Dm	913	Toccata prima ex Clave D manualiter	P 281	
Em	914	Toccata ex Eb manualiter		Copyist: H. N. Gerber
FM	540	Toccata col pedale obligato	P 803	Copyists: JTKrebs: 540/1 JLKrebs: 540/2
F♯m	910	Toccata ex Fis. Manualiter	ABB	Copyist: Hauptschreiber
GM	916	Toccata. Manualiter	ABB	Copyist: Hauptschreiber (and Nebenschreiber)
Gm	915	Toccata manualiter Gmol	P 1082	

Table IV
The Compass of the "Bach" Organs

Arnstadt (Neue Kirche)	manuals: CDE — d''' pedals: CDE — d'''
Mühlhausen (Divi Blasii)	manuals: CD — d''' pedals: CD — d'
Weimer (Schlosskirche)	manuals: C — c''' pedals: C — e'(?)
Köthen (Schlosskapelle)	manuals: C — e''' pedals: C — e'
Köthen (St. Agnus-kirche)	manuals: C — d''' (?) pedals: CD — d'e'f'
Leipzig*	manuals: CD — c''' pedals: CD — d'

(*The range observed in the organ works presumably composed during the Leipzig period.)

Table V

Keyboard Range of the Toccata, BWV 910-16

Work (BWV)	Key	Range
910	F# minor	C – B#) (b"
911	C minor	CD – c"
912/912a	D major	CDE – c"
913	D minor	CDE – c"
914	E minor	CD – c"
915	G minor	CD – c"
916	G major	CDE – c"

TOCCATA

d-moll

BWV 913

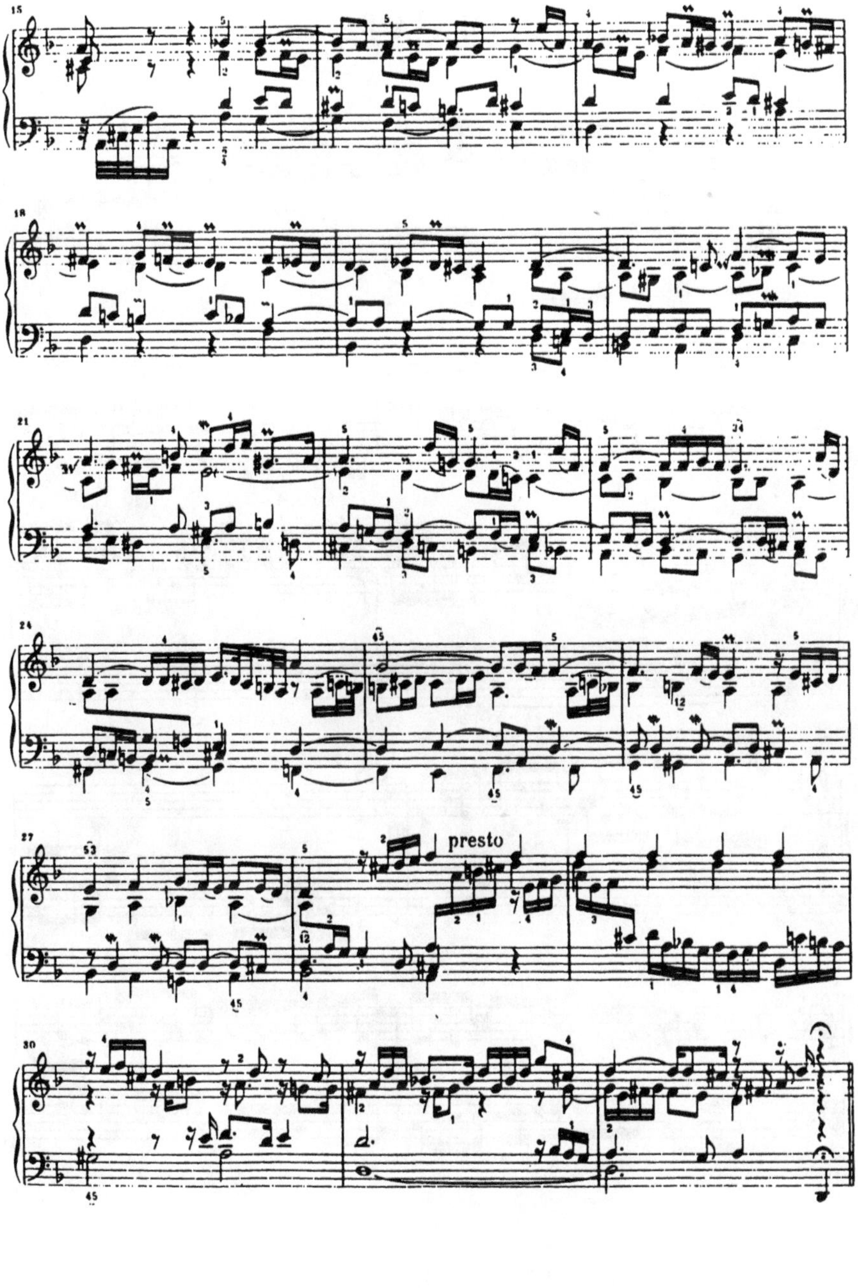
presto

TOCCATA

c-moll

BWV 911

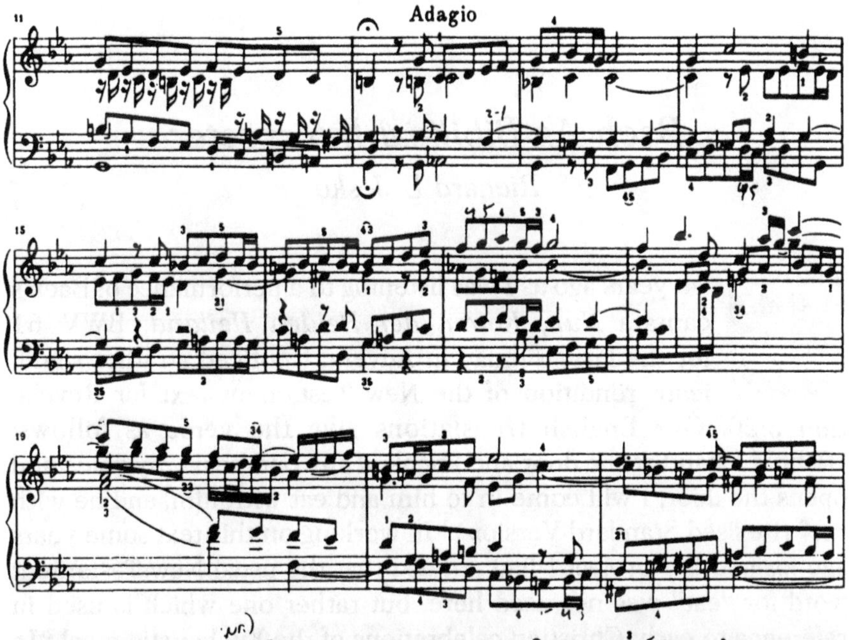
Adagio

Bach As Bibilical Interpreter

Richard L. Jeske

wo years ago as I was listening to a performance of Bach's cantata *Nun, Komm der Heiden Heiland*, BWV 61 for the First Sunday in Advent, I noticed a rather significant rendition of the New Testament text for Revelation 3:20. Our English translations give the verse as follows: "Behold I stand at the door and knock; if any one hears my voice and opens the door, I will come in to him and eat with him, and he with me" (Revised Standard Version).[1] In working on this text some years ago for another project I had noticed that the usual New Testament word for "eat" was not used here, but rather one which is used in reference to early Christian celebrations of the Eucharistic meal.[2] In the beautiful recitative in which Bach sets these words to music, the text reads: "Siehe, ich stehe vor der Tür und klopfe am. So jemand meine Stimme hören wird und die Tür auftun, zu dem werde ich eingehen und das Abendmahl mit ihm halten und er mit mir." ("Behold, I stand at the door and knock. If anyone hears my voice and opens the door I will go in and observe das Abendmahl with him. . . .") That the Lord's Supper is meant here is clearly shown by the previous aria, in which Jesus is asked to come to his church and to bless pulpit and altar, an obvious reference to Word and Sacrament.

It was such attention to the New Testament text which intrigued me, so much so that I decided to offer a course on "Bach and the New Testament" at the seminary where I teach. Of course, as amateurs quickly discover, this topic soon became more of a challenge than I had originally anticipated. Since Bach used librettists, to what extent could we speak of Bach and the New Testament? Perhaps, as in this case, Neumeister, or Franck, or Picander, *et al.* and the New Testament, but Bach and the New Testament? There were instances, of course, when Bach himself composed a text, but when could we be certain of such instances? There were times when he overruled his librettist, but when could those times be discovered? Faced with the intricacies which this topic now occasioned, I did the natural thing for an instructor feeling somewhat overwhelmed: I invited guest lecturers to teach my course! One of them, happily, was a man by the name of Michael Korn, who after his engrossing lecture on Bach's numerology convinced me that I should continue to pursue the present topic and offer a lecture in connection with the 1985 Festival. (Therefore all complaints about this presentation may properly be directed to him!) I would hope, however, that the following comments be understood as coming not from an expert musicologist, but from a teacher of New Testament who has had a lifelong attachment to the music of Johann Sebastian Bach.

The topic, "Bach as Biblical Interpreter," can be approached in various ways and raises a host of interesting questions. Of course, there is the question of Bach's musical interpretation of the biblical texts, a topic which continues to be dealt with frequently. Who can forget the repeated *Omnes* in the Magnificat, when Mary expresses her knowledge that all generations will call her blessed, or when the instruments stop abruptly at the end of the phrase, "the rich he has sent empty away"? We stand in amazement at Bach's ability to allow the music to realize the emotional and intellectual depths of a text, to draw attention to detail through tone painting, and to highlight the musical qualities of speech. The Yale New Testament scholar Paul Minear has written:

> Although Bach may not fully merit the title of the Fifth Evangelist, he can present excellent qualifications as an interpreter of all four Evangelists, first because he so frequently penetrated to the inner dynamics of the biblical narrative, and second, because he chose forms of expression that communicate those dynamics to a universal audience.[3]

Minear further makes the point that it has been wholly inappropriate to exclude Bach from histories of modern hermeneutics, and that the theological sciences suffer disaster when they are disjoined from music in particular, and indeed from other artistic forms of communication in general.[4]

Certainly it is clear that Bach's cantatas were originally meant to take part in the interpretation of a given biblical text, since the cantatas were designed for particular Sundays of the church year with their respective lectionary readings appointed for the day.

Therefore they fit into a long history of musical exposition which, as Alfred Dürr has shown, goes back to the Reformation and specifically to Luther himself.[5] It is Dürr's contention that Luther's theology resulted in a new orientation to church music, specifically Luther's conviction that the Word of God in the Scriptures remains dead and ineffective unless it is proclaimed. Since Luther, then, who himself composed hymnody and chant settings for the church's worship, the music of the church had its rightful place in the proclamation, and therefore in the interpretation, of the biblical text.[6] Dürr states that the history of church music from Schütz to Bach is therefore the history of the infusion of interpretive, expository elements into the music of the church's worship services.[7] The evolution of the cantata form is the history of the emergence of various musical forms—from motet to verse to madrigal to recitative and aria—to serve in the interpretive task within the context of the church's worship. Bach's cantatas then stand in a long musical tradition; but they stand also in a long tradition of biblical interpretation as well.

Our topic, however, is "Bach as Biblical Interpreter," and aside from the critical issue of the musical interpretation of texts there is the question of the wording in Bach's recitatives, arias, and chorals which also serve to interpret the biblical text. This necessarily involves us in the question of the librettists and their compositional procedures. What were their own theological dispositions? Did they receive instructions from Bach, and if so to what extent? But even more, since we know that at least two of Bach's librettists, namely Neumeister and Franck, were clergy themselves, what currents were at work in their training and in their contemporary setting which shaped their thinking and thus their compositions?[8] What interpretive methods were they following and in what controversies, if any, were they engaged?[9]

All these questions play a role in our ability to assess the work of Bach himself as a biblical interpreter. But on the margin are other issues as well, namely the important issue of Bach's relationship to Lutheran orthodoxy on the one hand and to Pietism on the other. Bach stood at the threshold of an important shift in religious disposition and observance, with seventeenth-century Lutheran orthodoxy's rigorous concentration on purity of doctrine and seventeenth- and eighteenth-century Pietism's reaction against cold religious formalism in favor of a subjective personal religious experiencing of the divine. Of course, we must not be too quick to caricature either of these movements with glib generalizations. Günther Stiller points out that Bach's Leipzig, "with its very conservative tradition, entirely in the mold of strict Lutheran orthodoxy, still represented a very vigorous world of faith."[10] Stiller also observes that the Lutheran Orthodoxy within which Bach worked resisted the pietistic distinction between sacred and secular, a distinction which we ourselves have not entirely abandoned, as can be shown by our reactions to hearing how Bach incorporated old drinking-songs and love-ballads into his sacred church works.[11]

It is therefore important to distinguish between elements of seventeenth- and eighteenth-century Pietism and elements which Bach received from his traditional church heritage. For instance, his close attention to the biblical text and his ability to understand it and articulate it musically cannot be seen as his involvement in pietistic renewal, but rather as part and parcel of liturgical life in early eighteenth-century Leipzig. While the city of Leipzig officially rejected Pietism, it built into its own public liturgical life a rigorous schedule of worship services which served to enhance prayer life and biblical literacy. Awareness of biblical content was shaped by the many opportunities for worship, complete with their corresponding number of sermons, which were available in the city during the course of each week of the church year. (We are told, by the way, that the proper length of the Sunday sermons was one hour—and that the weekday sermon should last no longer than one hour![12]) These sermons covered a wide range of biblical texts, and, judging from those examples still available to us, were extremely textual in content. There were the regular morning and afternoon services on Sundays and festival days in which the sermons expounded the traditional Gospel and Epistle readings for the day. At the Sunday afternoon service at St. Peter's church in Leipzig the practice began in 1712 of expounding the entire Bible from beginning to end, a tradition which continued throughout the eighteenth century. Besides these, however, there were sermons on entire books or connected chapters of the Old and New Testaments in the various weekday services, on the Passion of Jesus in the Sunday Vespers of Lent, and on Luther's Catechism in the Sunday Vespers of Advent. In addition, sermons on penitential texts were preached at Matins on Fridays and at Vespers on Saturdays, a reflection of the intensification of confessional practices in Leipzig.[13] Of course, the call to repentence was an important characteristic of Pietism, and its presence in Bach's music often strikes us as extremely pietistic.[14] But Bach's frequent use in his cantatas of hymns of penitence has its roots in traditional Lutheran confessional practice going back to Luther, whose theology occasioned frequent calls to repentance, not as an inner feeling but as an invitation to the hearer to recognize who he or she is before God, namely not a religious achiever but a recipient of God's mercy and grace. It is this theology, and not the theology of Pietism, which is behind the first person singular in the texts of Bach's church music. It is not the human being who is the object of inner spiritual and outer moral reshaping, but the human being who is being invited by the gospel toward new self-reflection and a renewed self-understanding.

Nor is the first person singular in Bach's cantata texts representative of the individualism of Pietism, which was critical—to the point of rejecting—the institutional forms of the church. To illustrate this we can turn again to the Advent Cantata #61, which in the spirit of the Advent season stresses Jesus' coming—first to the nations as born in flesh and blood, then to the church in Word and Sacrament, and only after that then finally to the individual believer. And here Jesus' coming is not in judgment as at the Last Day—which is another theme of Advent—but in his gracious invitation, "Behold I stand at the door and knock. . . ." This recitative, part four of Cantata BWV 61, is a poignant example of the combination of words and music to engage the hearer in Jesus' calling to the believer and to consider a response. Gilles Whittaker calls this brief ten-bar recitative "the gem of the cantata, indeed one of the most priceless treasures in them all. . . . Violins. . . , violas, and continuo maintain a steady progression of pizzicato chords, the gentle knocking of the Christ. . . , beginning with a strong yet soft dissonance, . . . and the voice . . . speaks gently. One can never think of the words without their association with the music. . . . No Italian masterpiece of painting brings Jesus so clearly before our eyes as these few bars of simple music."[15] It is not the Jesus who is to come as Judge at the end of time, but Jesus as the one who invites, gently, into fellowship with him. The response to this invitation is articulated in the following aria, with its eighth notes in the cello in an upward movement depicting an eager anticipation, even a running to meet the Savior.

My whole heart, open wide,
Jesus comes to draw within you.
    Though I soon be earth and ashes
    Me he never will disdain
    To see his joy in me
    That I become his dwelling
    Oh how blessed shall I always be!

In this aria the eschatological component of Advent is heard, namely that final time of the End when Jesus meets his own to be with them forever. There is nothing but quiet confidence expressed in this aria, and an absence of any fear whatsoever in view of the final Judgment. Again, an invitation is there for the hearer to take refuge in the good news of God's acceptance of the sinner, with full awareness of human mortality. This invitation is resolved in the final chorale, made up of only a portion of verse 7 of Philip Nicolai's hymn "How Brightly Shines the Morning Star": it is the Amen of the believing response of faith, again done with such firm confidence that one cannot help but answer the invitation by singing along:

> Amen, amen!
> Come, you beauteous crown of gladness! Do not tarry!
> Here I wait for you with longing!

It is this invitational character of the music of Bach that is so compellingly present in his church cantatas, and which in my opinion distinguishes Bach's music from the music of other great composers before him. It no longer suffices simply to bring musical interpretation to the biblical text, no matter how magnificent, colorful, or dramatic. The music must lay open the invitation of the text, the gospel invitation to the reader and the hearer to confront the claim of the text and to understand him- or herself anew in view of the grace of God. Earlier we mentioned Dürr's point that for Luther the Word of God in the Scriptures lies dead and ineffective unless it is proclaimed. This needs to be amplified a bit more. For Luther it was important for the preacher not simply to exposit the text, but to present the text as a vehicle for the proclamation of the gospel. This is the revolutionary component of Reformation hermeneutics.

When Luther embarked on his translation of the Bible into the German language, he published his New Testament version first, in 1522, complete with a set of prefaces to the various writings in the New Testament canon. As did Jerome's Latin Vulgate for centuries before him, Luther's prefaces included various historical and literary details about the various biblical writings, in fact some critical insights which came to be dealt with only centuries later. But the really new thing which Luther's prefaces offered was a comprehensive means by which the reader might examine and evaluate the biblical writings. That is, with his translation Luther was not interested simply in getting people to read the Bible; rather he was more interested in getting people to learn *how* to read it. His prefaces were designed to teach people what to look for when reading the New Testament, so that they, as he put it, "may not seek laws and commandments where (they) ought to be seeking the gospel and promises of God."[16] This is Luther's so-called "gospel hermeneutic," his principle that the purpose of reading the Scriptures is to find Christ there. It is this hermeneutical principle which Luther employed first of all as the means of evaluating the prefaces of the past. "See to it, therefore, that you do not make . . . a book of laws and doctrines out of the Gospel, as has been done heretofore and as certain prefaces put it, even those of St. Jerome."[17] For the first time in the history of preface writing a comprehensive methodological principle is proposed, a principle which for Luther came from within the biblical text itself rather than from the traditions surrounding it. This principle could now be used by the average reader to evaluate other introductory and interpretive opinions, and it is a principle which Luther put to work in evaluating the content of the New Testament itself. He invites the reader to use this principle in order to judge "all the books and decide among them which are the best," and the best books are the ones that reflect "the real nature of the gospel."[18] This is at the same time Luther's criticism of past prefaces and his reason for writing new ones, because "many unfounded (*wilde*) interpretations and prefaces have scattered the thought of Christians to a point where no one any longer knows what is gospel or law."[19]

It is furthermore interesting that Luther did not write prefaces for each of the four New Testament Gospels, but only one preface for them all. And even there his "gospel hermeneutic" is applied to the contents of the four Gospels: the descriptions of Jesus' miracles and actions are secondary to the message of his victory over sin, death, and hell—and therefore John's Gospel and Paul's letters are to be evaluated as "the foremost books": "for in them you do not find many works and miracles of Christ described, but you do find depicted in masterly fashion how faith in Christ overcomes sin, death, and hell, and gives life, righteousness, and salvation. This is the real nature of the gospel. . . ."[20] Therefore when Luther speaks of the Scriptures as the swaddling cloths and the manger in which Christ lies. . . ," and "lowly are these swaddling cloths, but dear is the treasure, Christ, who lies in them,"[21] the Christ which the reader is to find is not just any image of Christ present in the text. Not the miracle-working Christ but the Christ of the cross is the object of the biblical message and therefore the goal of every interpreter who desires to hear that message. Therefore not only each biblical writing is to be evaluated in the light of this message but each interpretation of it as well.

It seems apparent to me that Luther's approach to the biblical text is shared and promoted by Bach in terms of the consistent structure and content of his musical works. Of course, it is the interpretive and preaching tradition in which Bach stands, and although in reading the sermons of the late seventeenth and early eighteenth centuries one can see that this approach is not always followed—often there is still more law than gospel preached!—the cantatas of Bach look to the text for the day as the *vehicle* for the proclamation of the gospel. That is, the text for the day is not the object of the proclamation but the vehicle for it. Interpreters of Bach often comment with surprise how little reference is actually made at times in a given cantata to the text for the day. This is, however, only to be expected when we understand that the text is not the object but the vehicle of the proclamation.

This can be illustrated by the treatment of the Gospel lesson in Bach's four cantatas for the 16th Sunday after Trinity. The Gospel lesson for this day is the miracle-story in Luke 7:11-17, the story of Jesus' raising from death the son of the widow from Nain. Again, little reference is made at all to the story itself in these cantatas. All four cantatas (BWV 161, 95, 8, 27) concentrate instead on the believer's confrontation with death, on how death has lost its dread because of the death and resurrection of Christ, and how the believer looks forward to life with Christ after death. Allusions abound throughout the cantatas to other biblical and liturgical material. In the earliest of the four, composed in 1715 with Franck as the librettist, the opening chorale indicates the particular way in which biblical imagery is used:

Come, O death, thou sweetest hour,
When my soul
Tastes honey
From out of the mouth of the lion. . . .

The words allude to the story in the fourteenth chapter of the Book of Judges, in which Samson kills a lion and returns a few days later to find that in the carcass of the lion a swarm of bees had built a honeycomb, from which Samson then ate. Such a story is applied to the terror of death, which now has no terror but only sweetness because of the work of Christ. This particular use of biblical imagery has its roots in the Reformation preaching and interpretive tradition, as a sermon from the sixteenth century indicates:

> Since Samson found honey in the lion's mouth, he told a riddle in Judges 14:14. Sweetness came out of the terrifying. What is more terrifying than death, when it breaks your bones like a lion can (as Isaiah 38:13 says)? But still a Christian can find honey in the lion, and consolation in the hour of death.[22]

This example of the use of the Samson story as a vehicle for the preaching of the gospel of Christ's victory over death indicates the background for the kind of biblical interpretation we find in Bach's cantatas. Of course, perhaps there is a lack of direct reference to the story of the raising of the young man of Nain because these cantatas, with their theme of consolation in the face of death, were to be available for general use in funeral services. But the last of the four cantatas for Trinity 16, whose text was written in 1726 very possibly by Bach himself, moves beyond the treatment of death and grief simply as a topic for Christian reflection and instead confronts the hearer with his and her own mortality. The dialogical quality of the opening combined chorale and recitative poses the question: "Who knows how near to me my end is?" Interspersed after each line with recitative, the chorale's final line gives the answer: "My God, I pray through Christ's own blood, please allow that my end be good!" Throughout his cantata Bach does not allow the hearer to retreat into the distance as a bystander, but involves the hearer in a decision about his and her own existence. In all four cantatas there is the call to live eschatologically, that is not to allow the world and its values to determine one's existence. This use of the biblical text to confront the hearer existentially is exactly what the Reformation exegetical and homiletical tradition has brought to the task of biblical interpretation.

It is this refusal to let the hearer stand at a so-called objective distance that pervades the Passions and Oratorios. The "Jauchzet, frohlocket" at the beginning of the Christmas Oratorio introduces the hearer immediately into the action, namely into a response to the deed of God in the birth of Christ.

Be joyful, be glad! Praise these days!
Let us honor the name of Almighty God.

This sets the tone for the dialogical quality of the entire Christmas Oratorio, not only in terms of its text but also its structure. After the first recitative of the beginning of the Christmas story in Luke 2:1-6, the commentary in the next recitative, using language reminiscent of Cantata #140 on the parable of the wise and foolish maidens, calls to Zion to leave its weeping behind, because the seed of David and the star of Jacob has come. The alto aria, "Bereite dich, Zion," calls to Zion to prepare to meet the bridegroom. But it is not really clear who Zion is until the chorale answers with:

| Wie soll ich dich empfangen, | Lord, how shall I receive you? |
| Und wie begegn' ich dir? | How shall I greet you now? |

O aller Welt Verlangen,	You, the desire of all the world,
O meiner Seelen Zier!	You, the jewel of my own soul!
O Jesu, Jesu! setze	Lord Jesus, set down
Mir selbst die Fackel bei,	Your touch beside me here
Damit, was dich ergötze,	That your own will and pleasure
Mir kund und wissend sei.	Be now to me made clear.

The Zion of the Christmas Oratorio is not only the Jerusalem of the past, but also the present Jerusalem, namely the present hearers, who are no longer spectators in the Christmas drama, but participants who will be confronted with the claim of the biblical text.

It is this dialogical component that we find in so many of Bach's works, a component in which the claim of the text meets with a response from the hearer. One cannot help mentioning here the beautiful exchanges between the believer and Jesus in the *Wachet Auf* cantata, BWV 140:

Believer: When are you coming, my Salvation?

Jesus: I am coming, my Portion.

Believer: I'm waiting with my burning oil.

Believer and Jesus: (Now open/I open) the hall

Both: for the heavenly banquet. . . .

Believer: My friend is mine

Jesus: And I am thine

Both: Let love bring no division. . . .

Sometimes such dialogical exchanges indicate ambiguities, yes, the doubt which every person of faith has to contend with, as in Cantata #66, in which in an aria the alto and tenor voices represent both doubting and believing in the same lines: "I feared (in truth/not at all) the grave and all its darkness, And (complained/kept hope) that my salvation is (now/not) ripped away from me."

In the exegetical and interpretive tradition in which Bach stands, and in terms of his own professional vocation, we can now readily understand his desire to lay open the claim of the biblical text for the comtemporary hearer. Since his time exegesis and interpretation have insisted upon a historical-critical distance to ancient texts and have encouraged—and I would say necessarily so—that detached analysis which can provide as much objectivity as is humanly possible for descriptive exposition. But it is interesting that philosophical hermeneutics have begun now to come full circle, as articulated by Paul Ricoeur in his book *Interpretation Theory: Discourse and the Surplus of Meaning:*

Not the intention of the author, which is supposed to be hidden behind the text; not the historical situation common to the author and his original readers; not the expectations or feelings of these original readers; not even their understanding of themselves as historical and cultural phenomena. What has to be appropriated is the meaning of the text itself, conceived in a dynamic way as the direction of thought opened up by the text. In other words, what has to be appropriated is nothing other than the power of disclosing a world that constitutes the reference of the text . . . the disclosure of a possible way of looking at things, which is the genuine referential power of the text.[23]

If this is what interpretation of a text is all about, to open up a "direction of thought" which the text itself wishes to open, "the disclosure of a possible way of looking at things," then Bach would be at home in modern hermeneutical theory. For he, in his own work as an interpreter, again and again exhibits his interest in doing nothing other than disclosing the genuine referential power of the biblical text. And it is his ability to do so which ranks Bach among the most important interpreters of the biblical text in the entire Christian tradition.

Notes

1. *New English Bible:* "Here I stand knocking at the door; if anyone hears my voice and opens the door, I will come in and sit down to supper with him and he with me." *New American Bible:* "Here I stand, knocking at the door. If anyone hears me calling and opens the door, I will enter his house and have supper with him, and he with me." Today's English Version: "Listen! I stand at the door and knock; if anyone hears my voice and opens the door, I will come into his house and eat with him, and he will eat with me."

2. The general word for "eat" is *esthio,* while in Rev. 3:20 the word *deipnon* is used. Cf. 1 Corinthians 11:20, where *deipnon* designates the communal Eucharist.

3. Paul Minear, "J.S. Bach and J.A. Ernesti: A Case Study in Exegetical and Theological Conflict," in *Our Common History as Christians: Essays in Honor of Albert C. Outler,* ed. J. Deschner, L.T. Howe, & K. Penzel (N.Y.: Oxford U. Press, 1975), 152.

4. Ibid., 151.

5. Alfred Dürr, *Die Kantaten von Johann Sebastian Bach* (Kassel: Bärenreiter, 1971), 13ff.

6. Dürr points to the close connection between text and melody in Luther's hymns, e.g., the hymn "Isaiah Mighty Seer in Days of Old."

7. Dürr, ibid., 14.

8. Salomo Franck (1659-1725) was a secretary in the consistory at Weimar. Erdmann Neumeister (1671-1756), an orthodox Lutheran whose libretti show pietistic influences, was court preacher in Weissenfels from 1704-1715, when he became head pastor at the Jakobikirche in Hamburg. Other clergy who very likely served as librettists included the two chief pastors of Leipzig, Salomon Deyling and Christian Weiss. The layman Picander, a pen-name used by Christian Friedrich Henrici (1700-64), was a postal secretary and a tax collector in Leipzig who composed some 28 texts for Bach; many Bach scholars consider him a poor poet who nevertheless "could take directions from Bach and give him what he asked for" (Eva Mary Grew and Sydney Grew, *Bach* [NY: Collier Books, 1962], 182). Georg Christian Lehms (1684-1717), also a layperson, was the court poet at Darmstadt whose cantata texts Bach set to music in both Weimar and Leipzig (see Dürr, ibid., 28-29).

9. In her article "Bach's Kantatentexte in auslegungsgeschichtlicher Sicht," in *Bach als Ausleger der Bibel,* ed. by Martin Petzoldt (Göttingen: Vandenhoeck & Ruprecht, 1985), 17, Elke Axmacher makes the fascinating point that the Protestant librettists of Bach's cantatas still betray their indebtedness to the traditional pre-Reformation hermeneutic of the four-fold interpretation of Scripture, namely that a text must be analyzed for the purpose of discovering its literal, allegorical, moral, and mystical meanings. This means that Luther's rejection of this method of biblical interpretation was by no means automatically embraced throughout the Reformation churches!

10. G. Stiller, *Johann Sebastian Bach and Liturgical Life in Leipzig* (St. Louis: Concordia, 1984), 149. Originally published in German in 1970 Stiller's book is an important resource for understanding the practical religious context in which Bach lived and worked.

11. In the program notes to the Philadelphia Orchestra's performance of the *St. Matthew Passion* in March 1985, the word "pietistic" seems not to be used in any technical sense but rather to refer to anything religious (p. 20B). Of course, this is Bach for the concert hall. In Bach's Leipzig context, however, as Stiller (ibid., 100) points out, "only unfamiliarity with the true situation could have led to the view that all evidence of a life of piety had to be credited to Pietism and therefore had to be labeled as pietistic."

12. Stiller, ibid., 53, quoting *Leipziger Kirchen-Staat: Das ist, Deutlicher Unterricht vom Gottesdienst in Leipzig* (Leipzig, 1710) 7 and 40.

13. Stiller, ibid., 101.

14. For example, modern translators of the beautiful *Buss und Reu* aria in the *St. Matthew Passion* unfortunately push the text into an even more pietistic direction than the German words indicate:

Buss und Reu	Penitence and remorse
Knirscht das Sündenherz entzwei	Grind the sinful heart in two.
Dass die Tropfen meiner Zähren	May my teardrops
Angenehme Spezerei,	Bring welcome balm
Treuer Jesu, dir gebären.	To thee, trusty Jesus.
	(Tr. B. Jacobson, program notes,
	Philadelphia Orchestra, March. 1985)

Far less pietistic and sentimental is another translation:
Grief for sin
Rends the guilty heart within
May my weeping and my mourning
Be a welcome sacrifice.
Loving Saviour, hear in mercy.
(Tr. J. Lyons, for the Westminster Recording of 1956, H. Scherchen, cond. Symphony Orchestra and Chorus)
It is important that this aria be seen as having a part in the exposition of the text of the anointing at Bethany (Matthew 26:6-13); however, it is not simply a descriptive exposition but a kerygmatic invitation to the hearer to engage in that self-reflection which results in repentance. Repentance is not a pietistic feeling that might lead to moralistic transformation, but a new self-understanding in view of the gospel of God's mercy in Christ.

15. W. Gilles Whittaker, *The Cantatas of Johann Sebastian Bach: Sacred and Secular,* Vol. I (London: Oxford U. Press, (1959) 1981; 149.

16. *Luther's Works,* Vol. 35 (Philadelphia: Fortress, 1960), 357.

17. Ibid., 360.

18. Ibid., 361.

19. Ibid., 357.

20. Ibid., 362.

21. Ibid., 236.

22. Heinrich Müller, *Evangelische Herzenspiegel* (1679), as quoted in Elke Axmacher, "Bachs Kantatentexte in auslegungsgeschichtlicher Sicht," in *Bach als Ausleger der Bibel,* ed. Martin Petzoldt (Göttingen: Vandenhoeck & Ruprecht, 1985), 15.

23. Paul Ricoeur, *Interpretation Theory: Discourse and the Surplus of Meaning* (Fort Worth: Texas Christian U. Press, 1976), 92.

www.ingramcontent.com/pod-product-compliance
Lightning Source LLC
Chambersburg PA
CBHW050349110426
42812CB00008B/2414